Bar

USA

Atlantic Ocean

Miami

BAHAMAS

CUBA

JAMAICA

DOMINICAN
REPUBLIC

HAITI

PUERTO
RICO

Caribbean Sea

BARBADOS

SOUTH AMERICA

Douglas McCreath

HarperCollins*Publishers*

This book was produced using QuarkXPress™ and
Adobe Illustrator 88™ on Apple Macintosh™ computers
and output to separated film on a Linotronic™ 300 Imagesetter

Text: Douglas McCreath
Images: Portfolios Photography
Electronic Cartography: Susan Harvey Design
Design: Ted Carden

First published 1991
Copyright © HarperCollins Publishers
Published by HarperCollins Publishers
Printed in Hong Kong
ISBN 0 00 435757-4

HOW TO USE THIS BOOK

Your Collins Traveller Guide will help you find your way around your holiday destination quickly and easily. It is split into two sections which are colour-coded:

The blue section provides you with an alphabetical sequence of headings, from **BEACHES** to **WHAT TO SEE** via **EXCURSIONS**, **RESTAURANTS**, **SHOPPING** etc. Each entry within a topic includes information on how to get there, how much it will cost you, when it will be open and what to expect. Furthermore, every page has its own map showing the position of each item and the nearest landmark. This allows you to orientate yourself quickly and easily in your new surroundings.

To find what you want to do – having dinner, visiting a museum, going for a walk or shopping for gifts – simply flick through the blue headings and take your pick!

The red section is an alphabetical list of information. It provides essential facts about places and cultural items – 'What are Chattel Houses?', 'When is Crop Over?', 'Where is Baxter's Road?' – and expands on subjects touched on in the first half of the book. This section also contains practical travel information. It ranges through how to find accommodation, where to hire a car, the variety of eating places and food available, tips on health, information on money, which newspapers are available, how to find a taxi and where the youth hostels are. It is lively and informative and easy to use. Each band shows the first three letters of the first entry on the page. Simply flick through the bands till you find the entry you need!

All the main entries are also cross-referenced to help you find them. Names in small capitals – **NIGHTLIFE** – tell you that there is more information about the item you are looking for under the topic on nightlife in the first part of the book. So when you read 'see **NIGHTLIFE**' you turn to the blue heading for **NIGHTLIFE**. The instruction 'see **A-Z**' after a word lets you know that the word has its own entry in the second part of the book. Similarly words in bold type – **Garrison Savannah** – also let you know that there is an entry in the A-Z for the indicated name. In both cases you just look under the appropriate heading in the red section. Packed full of information and easy to use – you'll always know where you are with your Collins Traveller Guide!

James Street

Highway 3

Milk Market

WATERFRONT CAFÉ

High Street

Broad Street

St. Michael's Row

Bridge Street

Highway 1

Cavans Lane

HERMAN'S WHARF

BROWN SUGAR

BRIDGETOWN

Bay Street

Atlantic Ocean

T. JOHN

ST. PHILIP

CRANE BEACH HOTEL RESTAURANT

INTRODUCTION

Escape, just for a few moments, from all those well-worn clichés, cast yourself adrift from troubled thoughts, and let your mind float in a voyage of adventure as you seek a far-away island of treasures and soothing promises of peace and tranquillity. Then imagine yourself relaxing beneath a palm tree, shaded from the warm tropical sunshine, cool drink in hand as you gaze lazily towards the aquamarine sea gently spilling over the deserted coral-white sands spread before you. But don't pinch yourself yet, because if it's fun to dream, it's bliss to experience, and turning stereotype into reality is quite simple when you discover a Caribbean jewel like Barbados.

People have been discovering Barbados for a long time now. The first Europeans to visit were Spanish and Portuguese traders in the 16thC, but they didn't stay. It was an Englishman, Captain John Powell, who claimed the island for the Crown in 1625, and it remained a colony until Independence in 1966. The first settlers arrived from England in 1627, landing at Holetown to find an uninhabited island of only 166 square miles, densely covered in thick vegetation. As clearing began, they planted spices, tobacco, cotton and sugar, a crop which was to dominate the economy for over three centuries. But tourism has now replaced sugar as Barbados' chief business, and it is indicative of the country's political stability and well-defined infrastructure that this transfer has come about without either rancour or environmental upheaval.

Today's discoverers come from all over the world, especially from Europe and North America, and in no time they can identify Barbados' long association with Britain through place names such as Dover, Worthing, Brighton or Folkestone, not to mention the Scotland District of St. Andrew, or Nelson's Statue in Trafalgar Square, erected some 30 years in advance of its counterpart in London. And there are early

American connections too – George Washington visited in 1751, staying for seven weeks, and even before then strong links had been forged with Carolina, with several Barbadians leaving to settle there. However, the island was, throughout its colonial history, inextricably influenced by Britain's fortunes both at home and abroad, and legacies are evident in such diversities as ecclesiastical and military architecture, the democratic system of government, and even in the people, some of them

descendents of those punished for their alleged parts in the English Civil War, the Duke of Monmouth's revolt or the Jacobite rebellions. For a fascinating journey into the past, a visit to the Barbados Museum is very rewarding. There you can learn much about the island's heritage, natural history, people and culture.

But the principal features which draw so many visitors to Barbados are, of course, the enviable combinations of agreeable climate, an abundance of superb beaches, and beautiful scenery. Everybody is catered for, whether they seek total relaxation, active recreation or a bit of both, and the absolute lack of pressure to decide what, where and when just adds to the relaxed ambience of the place. For the passive there are, even on this small island, some quiet beaches to be found off the beaten track where you might not see another person all day or, if that is not inspiring enough, there is no shortage of interesting places to visit, from plantation Great Houses to caves. For those who enjoy some action, the extensive menu of activities includes anything from an organized morning walk to scuba diving for sunken artefacts around a shipwreck.

But it is the climate which dominates everything – eight or nine hours of sunshine on most days, with the temperature rarely rising above 30°C, or falling below 23°C, and a steady, cooling breeze to keep excesses at bay. The people are pleasant too, and are always willing to lend helpful advice or friendly assistance when asked. They are courteous by nature and expect the same respect in return. Their language is English, but their dialect incorporates distinctly Bajan words which to the untrained ear may at times be difficult to follow.

First-time visitors are frequently surprised by the contrasting scenic qualities of Barbados, which crams an astonishing variety of beautiful countryside and spectacular coastline into its small area. Predominantly a coral island, just under a fifth of the terrain is made up of clay and sandstone deposits which have shaped the northeastern part into hills (in some places reaching over 1000 ft) with

steep valleys nestling below. The views from these heights, particularly over the east coast, are stunning. While guided tours around the island by bus or taxi are readily available, many people prefer to hire a car to explore at their own pace such features as the crashing Atlantic surf at North Point, the sheltered west coastal areas, the wild landscape of the east coast or the gentle, rolling, lush vegetation to the south. Barbados is divided into 11 parishes, each with its own parish church, and the boundaries have remained virtually unchanged since 1645. The population of about 254,000 is well spread over the island, and dotted about everywhere are little villages with their colourfully painted chattel houses and nearby cricket field.

Accommodation facilities are varied and generally of a good standard,

ranging from top international hotels to small, self-catering apartments.
It is also possible to rent houses and villas, complete with maid service
and cook. Most of the hotels and apartments are stretched along the
west and south coasts, and while they usually have their own pool, a
beach is rarely far away. Bridgetown, the bustling capital, is located in
the southwest corner of the island and is easily reached from either
coast by car, taxi or bus. There you will find plenty of duty-free shops,
restaurants, markets and noisy stall vendors offering local delicacies,
fruits and drinks. Shopping centres are also located in the main residen-
tial areas, and supermarkets are well stocked with produce from home
and abroad.

Whether your day has been spent exploring the countryside or just
idling on the beach, make sure you have plenty of energy left to enjoy
the evening ahead. As the sun sets, and the sounds of whistling tree

frogs and crickets begin to fill the sky, it is time to sit back and savour a rum cocktail as you take your pick from the rich feast of entertainment open to you. There is no lack of choice whatever your budget or preference: be it to dine and dance under the stars, an evening cruise, a nightclub, a show or a disco, you are certain to find fun and enjoyment. Wherever you go music will be heard, unfolding another aspect of Barbadian culture with *tuk* bands, calypsonians and steel bands pounding the airwaves. The calypso has roots in songs brought from Africa by the slaves, and today's lyrics are often used as much for political comment as for entertainment. Jazz also is popular and is featured in a number of nightspots. Some of the best restaurants in the Caribbean are found in Barbados, offering superb local and international cuisine, while at the other end of the scale is Baxter's Road in Bridgetown – known as 'The Street That Never Sleeps', where Bajan delicacies are sold from stalls, and music throbs till dawn.

After a few days, as the island and its lifestyle become more familiar, you will still be enchanted by the sight of coconut palms swaying in a gentle breeze, the shimmering sea, sweet fragrances from tropical flowers, the shrieks of monkeys, and the clear sky, brilliant by day, a star-studded canopy by night. Can it really be true or has the image become a mirage? Has that earlier dream simply faded into fantasy or

does Barbados really provide such sumptuous prizes? Perhaps the answer lies with the thousands of visitors who return time and again to this beautiful island in the sun, so why not join in the escape and discover some of its treasures for yourself?

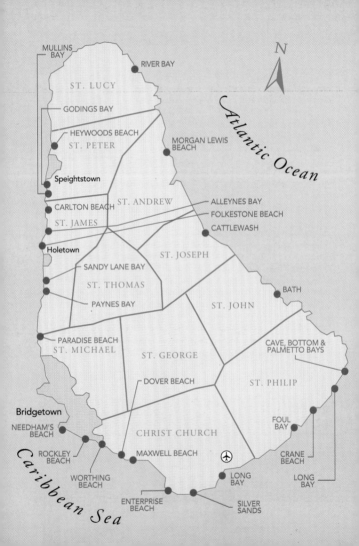

MULLINS BAY

RIVER BAY

ST. LUCY

Atlantic Ocean

GODINGS BAY

HEYWOODS BEACH

ST. PETER

MORGAN LEWIS BEACH

Speightstown

CARLTON BEACH

ST. ANDREW

ALLEYNES BAY

FOLKESTONE BEACH

ST. JAMES

CATTLEWASH

Holetown

ST. JOSEPH

SANDY LANE BAY

ST. THOMAS

BATH

PAYNES BAY

ST. JOHN

PARADISE BEACH

ST. MICHAEL

CAVE, BOTTOM & PALMETTO BAYS

ST. GEORGE

ST. PHILIP

DOVER BEACH

Bridgetown

FOUL BAY

NEEDHAM'S BEACH

CHRIST CHURCH

ROCKLEY BEACH

MAXWELL BEACH

CRANE BEACH

WORTHING BEACH

LONG BAY

ENTERPRISE BEACH

LONG BAY

SILVER SANDS

Caribbean Sea

N

HEYWOODS BEACH St. Peter.
Next to Heywoods Resort, this is a fine, long, gently sloping beach. There is a lifeguard station and water-sports centre, with hotel facilities nearby.

GODINGS BAY St. Peter.
Cobblers Cove Hotel is situated close to this relatively peaceful stretch of tree-lined beach. There are water-sports facilities in the vicinity.

MULLINS BAY St. Peter.
A popular area offering safe bathing in calm waters. Beach vendors are prevalent here, and a small bar and restaurant adjoin the beach.

CARLTON BEACH St. James.
An unspoiled beach fringed by small houses. What it lacks in facilities it gains in solitude despite proximity to the main road. See EXCURSION 1*.*

ALLEYNES BAY St. James.
The excellent beaches here consist of fine, coral sand and there is a public-access point next to the Colony Club, one of several first-class hotels on this coast. Most offer water sports as well as bar and dining facilities.

FOLKESTONE BEACH St. James.
Offshore reefs make this a popular place to snorkel. The pleasant beach has a lifeguard station, with water-sports facilities nearby.

SANDY LANE BAY St. James.
With a wide expanse of fine sand gently shelving into the placid sea, this is a tranquil spot. Public access point just south of Sandy Lane Hotel.

PAYNES BAY St. James.
A lengthy area of quality beach with two good hotels close by: Treasure Beach and Tamarind Cove, where you can buy refreshments and meals.

PARADISE BEACH St. James.
A very popular spot with half a mile of beautiful white sand. The Paradise Beach Club Hotel offers full facilities, with water sports also available.

NEEDHAM'S BEACH Below Hilton Hotel, St. Michael.
A vast beach at the southwestern corner of the island. Numerous water sports can be arranged from the centre on the beach.

ROCKLEY BEACH Adjacent to Accra Beach Hotel, Christ Church.
This beach is popular with both visitors and locals enjoying the surf and fine sands. Beachwear and souvenirs are for sale at stalls by the car park, and there is a pizzeria close by. Lifeguards are on duty. See **EXCURSION 2**.

WORTHING BEACH Christ Church.
A short distance to the east of Rockley (see above), this beach is, by contrast, much quieter, but lacks any significant facilities. Protruding reefs just offshore mean that swimming is limited to fairly shallow waters.

DOVER BEACH Christ Church.
This popular beach, towards the eastern end of St. Lawrence Gap, is well served by nearby hotels and restaurants. There is a lifeguard station and water-sports facilities. Stalls at the car park sell beachwear and T-shirts.

MAXWELL BEACH West end of Maxwell Coast Rd, Christ Church.
This pleasant beach of tree-fringed white sands has a lifeguard station but limited facilities. Reached by a track beside the Ambrosia Restaurant.

ENTERPRISE BEACH Christ Church.
A comparatively sheltered beach (also known as Miami Beach), this is very popular with locals. It has a picnic area and lifeguards on duty.

SILVER SANDS Christ Church.
The seas here are a Mecca for windsurfers, but swimmers must be wary of currents and tidal conditions. The beach is of beautiful, fine, white sand, and the Silver Sands Hotel has a beach bar and restaurant.

LONG BAY Christ Church.
Often completely empty, this excellent beach runs northwest for nearly a mile from Inch Marlowe Point. It lacks facilities of any kind, including shade. Be wary of currents and remember there are no lifeguards nearby.

FOUL BAY St. Philip.
Contrary to its name this is a beautiful, cliff-lined bay with lovely, white sands, but with no facilities. Road signs indicate access. See **Beaches**.

CRANE BEACH St. Philip.
Running north from the Crane Beach Hotel, this long beach is interrupted by rocky promontories which can be scaled by steps. See **Beaches**.

LONG BAY St. Philip.
Lying below Sam Lord's Castle (see **A-Z***), this bay has superb beaches among coral cliffs and rocks. Coconut palms give shade. See* **Beaches**.

CAVE, BOTTOM & PALMETTO BAYS St. Philip.
Three picturesque little bays with white, half-moon-shaped beaches. All are surrounded on three sides by steep cliffs, and paths and steps descend to the sands. Access to Cave Bay is via Harrismith's, to Bottom Bay via Apple Hall, and for Palmetto Bay you should follow signs to Peat Bay. There are no facilities at any of these beaches. See **Beaches**.

BATH North of Conset Bay, St. John.
This is a splendid, wide beach fringed with trees and beach houses. Tables provided for picnicking are among the few facilities. See **Beaches**.

CATTLEWASH St. Joseph.
This is a wild and spectacular beach which stretches northwards for over two miles beneath a backdrop of towering hills. There are facilities at the Kingsley Club, and the beach has a lifeguard station. See **Beaches**.

MORGAN LEWIS BEACH St. Andrew.
This beautiful, unspoiled spot, very popular with locals, is reached by a mile-long track starting just south of Morgan Lewis Mill. See **Beaches**.

RIVER BAY St. Lucy.
A very scenic inlet with a small, sandy cove protected from breakers as they crash into the surrounding bluffs. No swimming is allowed but parking, picnic areas and toilets are all provided. See **Beaches**.

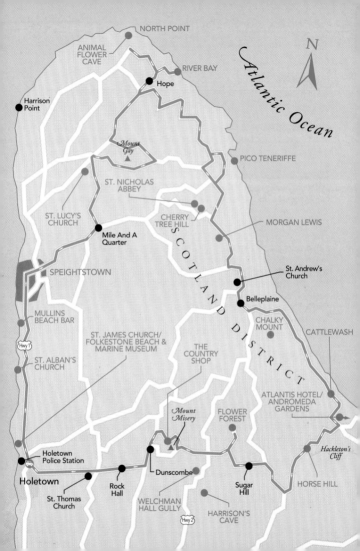

N

Atlantic Ocean

NORTH POINT

ANIMAL FLOWER CAVE

RIVER BAY

Hope

Harrison Point

Mount Gay

PICO TENERIFFE

ST. NICHOLAS ABBEY

ST. LUCY'S CHURCH

CHERRY TREE HILL

MORGAN LEWIS

Mile And A Quarter

St. Andrew's Church

SPEIGHTSTOWN

Belleplaine

S C O T L A N D   D I S T R I C T

CHALKY MOUNT

CATTLEWASH

MULLINS BEACH BAR

Hwy 1

ST. JAMES CHURCH/ FOLKESTONE BEACH & MARINE MUSEUM

THE COUNTRY SHOP

ST. ALBAN'S CHURCH

ATLANTIS HOTEL/ ANDROMEDA GARDENS

Mount Misery

FLOWER FOREST

Hackleton's Cliff

Holetown Police Station

Holetown

Dunscombe

Rock Hall

St. Thomas Church

Sugar Hill

HORSE HILL

WELCHMAN HALL GULLY

HARRISON'S CAVE

Hwy 2

EXCURSION 1

A 40-mile drive along the scenic coast and countryside of the northern parishes: St. James, St. Peter, St. Lucy, St. Andrew, St. Joseph and St. Thomas.

Start at Holetown Police Station in St. James (see **Holetown**), a fitting point from which to begin – as you will see from the nearby monument, this was where Englishmen first landed on the island in 1625 (although the date on the plaque erroneously states 1605!). Head out of town going north along Highway 1.

0.5 mile – St. James Church (see **A-Z**). A road on the left-hand side leads to the church which stands on the site of the original building dating from the mid 1600s. It contains many interesting antiquities. Folkestone Beach (see **BEACHES 1**) and the Marine Museum (see **WHAT TO SEE 2**) are nearby.

Rejoin Highway 1 and continue north, passing on the left some of the island's grandest beach hotels – Coral Reef Club, Colony Club, Glitter Bay and the Royal Pavilion, as well as the neat little chattel houses (see **A-Z**) strung out along the roadside.

2.6 miles – St. Alban's Church. You can gain access here to the normally quiet Carlton Beach (see **BEACHES 1**).

3.7 miles – Mullins Beach Bar. The bar sits poised above the sandy bay from which it takes its name (see **BEACHES 1**). Continue north.

4.3 miles – Speightstown (see **A-Z**). The town is off to the left, and the signposted road will take you into the town centre. Speightstown was at one time known as Little Bristol because of its close trading links with the English town and despite some modern development, a few of its unique three-storied 18thC buildings remain. The Georgian-style St. Peter's Church, rebuilt a number of times following destruction by hurricanes and fires, dates originally from 1629. Go past the church, keeping it on your

Speightstown

right, until you reach Major Walk Rd. Turn right and on reaching the junction at the bus terminal, turn right then left at the traffic lights to head for the town of Mile And A Quarter on Highway 1. En route you will pass through a landscape of cane fields, gullies and palm trees. From Mile And A Quarter, follow the signs to St. Lucy's Church, located by a roundabout two miles away and 9.1 miles from the start. The first church on this site was built in 1629, and this, the fourth, was constructed in 1837 in Georgian style. Take the road opposite the church, signposted for Mount Gay, and soon you are ascending a twisty road giving pleasant views over sugar-cane plantations towards the lighthouse at Harrison Point and the Caribbean Sea.

At 10.2 miles you will come to a sign indicating the famous Mount Gay Rum Refinery (see **Tours**) down a short cul-de-sac on the left, where free guided tours are available.

At 11.6 miles, turn left at the sign marked 'River Bay, Archer's Bay, Nesfield' and proceed along a narrow road between cane fields. You will get occasional glimpses of the distant coastline sweeping around the north of the island. On reaching a T-junction a mile and a half along this road turn right, and a third of a

mile further on fork left in the direction of River Bay (you can make a detour from the excursion route to Animal Flower Cave – see **WHAT TO SEE 2**, **A-Z** – and North Point). Travelling on for another 1.8 miles you will come to the village of Hope, where you should turn right at the Y-junction.

15.5 miles – **River Bay**. A picturesque part of the northeast coastline, with a bracing seascape.

The next part of this excursion, through some pretty villages, involves much twisting and turning but patience should reward you with an interesting cameo of rural Bajan life.

Retrace your steps back through Hope, turning left at the junction, and proceed for almost three quarters of a mile to turn left at the sign marked 'Cove, Pie Corner, Spring Garden'. This narrow road bends right before reaching a T-junction at 17.8 miles. Turn left towards St. Clements and, just under a mile further on, turn right at the sign reading 'Boscobelle, Morgan Lewis via Pie Corner'. 0.4 of a mile after this, turn left at the T-junction at the sign reading 'St. Clements Church, Cove Bay, Boscobelle, Morgan Lewis'. Proceed down the hill for almost half a mile and turn right at the sign for 'Cove via Pie Corner'. Your accumulated mileage from the start should now read 19.3 miles. Carry on the short distance to a sign pointing left to Cove Bay (you can make a detour down this road – which later becomes a track – to view the scenic coastline and Pico Teneriffe, a prominent landmark, in the shape of a pillar of rock, at the top of cliffs to the south).

Continuing past the sign to Cove Bay, keep straight on up the hill and at 20.7 miles turn left at the sign marked 'Farley Hill, Cherry Tree Hill, Morgan Lewis, East Coast Road'. The road now descends steeply towards another junction half a mile further on where you keep left. Over the next mile or so, magnificent views of the Atlantic coastline far below unfold. On reaching the next T-junction at 22.4 miles, turn left (although if you prefer, you can turn right here to get to St. Nicholas Abbey – see **WHAT TO SEE 2**, **A-Z** – via Cherry Tree Hill) and the scenery now additionally embraces the Scotland District.

22.9 miles – **Morgan Lewis** (see **WHAT TO SEE 2**). A fully restored windmill owned by the Barbados National Trust (see **A-Z**) with an interesting museum where exhibits explain the history of sugar mills.

Now you are almost back at sea level. Carry straight on, ignoring Charles O'Neal Highway on the right and when you come to St. Andrew's Church, turn left for Belleplaine from where there is a good view of Chalky Mount (see **WHAT TO SEE 2**). In contrast to the coral features found elsewhere in Barbados, this part of the island consists of clay deposits and many potteries operate around the heights of Chalky Mount. In Belleplaine turn left on to the signposted 'East Coast Road' which for over three miles sweeps alongside a dramatic vista of sea, surf and beaches to the left, and steep hills on the right.

28.5 miles – **Cattlewash**. See **BEACHES 3**.

From here the road climbs as it turns inland and you should initially follow directions reading 'Edgewater Hotel' and 'Andromeda Gardens' looking out after almost a mile for the sign to Bridgetown at the top of the hill where you should turn right (if you prefer, you can make a detour here and carry straight on to get to Atlantis Hotel – see **MUSTS** – and Andromeda Gardens – see **PARKS & GARDENS**).

Barbados National Trust
BUILDING
OF
HISTORIC
INTEREST

The road now begins to climb steeply, affording good views northward just after the Joe's River area. At St. Joseph's village keep right at the junction (you can get to Cotton Tower – see WHAT TO SEE 3, **Signal Stations** – by turning left here).

31.2 miles – Horse Hill. From here there are superb views, and you can see right over to the west coast. Keeping straight on for 0.7 of a mile, look out for a sign to 'Flower Forest' where you should turn right. Half a mile up the road follow the sign 'Todd's Corner via Chimborazo', and very shortly after this turn left at the fork on the top of the hill where your cumulative mileage will now be 32.7 miles. Carry on through Sugar Hill, with no deviations until you reach a T-junction at 33.6 miles showing Flower Forest to the right, where you also turn right.

34.1 miles – Flower Forest. The entrance to the beautiful tropical gardens (see MUSTS) lies here. If you are not going in you should turn left, following the signs reading 'Barbados Wildlife Reserve'.

Just under a mile further on you will come to a junction. Off to the left are Harrison's Cave (see MUSTS) and the southern entrance to Welchman Hall Gully (see PARKS & GARDENS). You can deviate from the route of the excursion to visit these; otherwise turn right, following signs marked 'H'way 2 – East Coast Road, Farley Hill', then left at the junction just ahead and shortly after you will pass the north entrance to Welchman Hall Gully. Proceed now towards the radio tower which sits at the top of Mount Misery.

35.8 miles – The Country Shop. A variety of local handicrafts is on sale here (see **Arts & Crafts**). Follow the road towards the village of Dunscombe, about a mile further on. As you descend there are excellent views over the west coast of the island, with the Caribbean Sea beyond. At Dunscombe turn left at the junction, and follow the road towards Edge Hill for a mile and a half to an unmarked junction where you turn right, towards the sea. On the way you pass through a landscape of gullies, glades and lush vegetation.

The road now drops steadily and after passing through Rock Hall village, turn right at the minor junction, then proceed a very short distance to a T-junction where you turn left then immediately right by St. Thomas Church. Holetown is reached after two miles at a junction opposite Jamestown Pharmacy, close to the monument from where you started.

Flower Forest

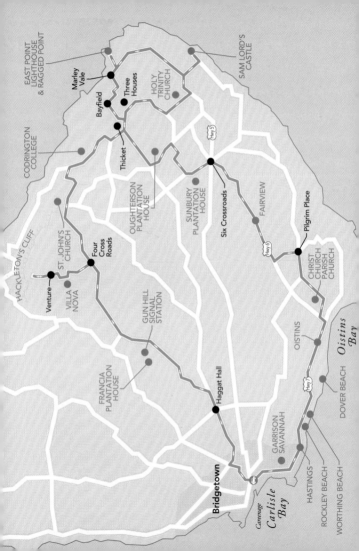

EAST POINT
LIGHTHOUSE
& RAGGED POINT

SAM LORD'S
CASTLE

Marley
Vale

Three
Houses

Bayfield

HOLY
TRINITY
CHURCH

CODRINGTON
COLLEGE

Thicket

hwy 5

OUGHTERSON
PLANTATION
HOUSE

SUNBURY
PLANTATION
HOUSE

FAIRVIEW

Six Crossroads

Pilgrim Place

HACKLETON'S CLIFF

ST. JOHN'S
CHURCH

Four
Cross
Roads

hwy 6

CHRIST
CHURCH
PARISH
CHURCH

Venture

VILLA
NOVA

GUN HILL
SIGNAL
STATION

OISTINS

Oistins
Bay

FRANCIA
PLANTATION
HOUSE

Haggat Hall

DOVER BEACH

hwy 7

GARRISON
SAVANNAH

Bridgetown

HASTINGS

ROCKLEY BEACH

WORTHING BEACH

Careenage
Carlisle
Bay

A 50-mile drive taking in plantation houses, churches, a castle, and the beautiful, rolling countryside of the southern parishes: Christ Church, St. Philip, St. John and St. George.

Starting from the Careenage (see **WHAT TO SEE 1**) in Bridgetown, leave the city on Highway 7 heading towards Hastings and shortly, on the right-hand side, you will see the shimmering turquoise waters of Carlisle Bay sweeping round to Needham's Point, site of the Hilton Hotel.

1.4 miles – Garrison Savannah (see **WHAT TO SEE 1**, **A-Z**). A racecourse has now been built here. There is still some evidence of Barbados' military past in the form of buildings and an interesting cannon collection in front of the old Guard House. The Barbados Museum (see **A-Z**) is located on the far side of the Savannah. Continue along the main road, past the pretty villas of  Hastings, which was originally created in the 1820s as the island's first seaside resort. Proceed on through the suburbs of Rockley, with its popular beach (see **BEACHES 2**), followed by Worthing (see **BEACHES 2**), then Dover (see **BEACHES 2**), where at the roundabout you should take the second exit towards Oistins.

6 miles – Oistins. On reaching the fishing port (see **Events**, **Oistins**), turn left at Oistins Hill, ascending only a short distance to a minor crossroads, where you turn sharp right. Along this road, just past Foundation School, is Christ Church Parish Church. The churchyard contains the eerie Chase Vaults (see **A-Z**), scene of unexplained happenings in the 19thC. Pleasant views of the south-coast area can be had further along this road. At the stop sign at the end, turn left up Thornbury Hill, continuing until you reach the service station at Pilgrim Place, then turn left into Lowland Rd. Cross straight over the Tom Adams Highway, a quarter of a mile up this road and, after passing the mattress factory on the left, turn right at the junction with Highway 6,

following the sign for 'Six Crossroads'. The route now passes through large sugar-cane fields, hamlets of chattel houses (see **A-Z**) and banana plantations.

10.5 miles – Fairview. From this village, a rural panorama unfolds over to the southeast coast ahead of you. Cross straight over the junction, past the village, and 1.5 miles further on, the road bends left just before reaching the Four Square sugar factory and is signposted 'Six Crossroads'. At Six Crossroads take the second exit from the left, and follow signs which read 'Sunbury Plantation House'.

13.6 miles – Sunbury Plantation House. This 300-year-old mansion (**WHAT TO SEE 4**, **A-Z**) is a superb example of the island's great plantation houses. It has a restaurant and bar. On leaving, turn left at the exit gate and then take the first turning on the right, following a winding road through more cane fields for just over a mile, until reaching a T-junction where you turn left towards Oughterson House Zoo Park which is three quarters of a mile up this road on the right-hand side.

15.5 miles – Oughterson Plantation House. This building, which dates from the 1700s, is open daily. Barbados Zoo Park (see **WHAT TO SEE 4**) is in the grounds. On leaving the park turn right and at the T-junction a short distance ahead, turn right again, following the signs for Codrington College. As you proceed down this road, East Point Lighthouse comes into view. Go straight on at the junction about a mile further on, following, for the moment, the sign to King George V Park, but at the junction at Three Houses Park a short distance away, turn left for East Point. The road now bends its way to Bayfield, and there you should follow the sign to Bridgetown via Marley Vale.

On arriving at Marley Vale go up the hill through the village and you will see the lighthouse straight ahead, signposted 'Ragged Point'.

20 miles – East Point Lighthouse & Ragged Point. The peninsula here offers very good views of the rugged southeast coastline, with its cliff-lined bays and crashing Atlantic surf. Retrace your steps back to Marley Vale, then turn left to follow directions to Six Crossroads for two and a half miles, and take another left turn at the sign to Sam Lord's Castle. At the T-junction at the bottom of this road, turn left.

24.5 miles – Sam Lord's Castle (see **WHAT TO SEE 4**, **A-Z**). The building is now a luxury resort hotel. A number of antiques which once belonged to the mansion's original resident, a reputed smuggler, can be seen inside. This is a lovely place to stop for a cooling drink.

On leaving Sam Lord's Castle take the first turning on the right, signposted 'H'way 5 via Long Bay', and at the T-junction at the top of the road turn left at the sign reading 'Six Crossroads, Bridgetown'. Follow this road for a short distance until you come to a sign marked 'Holy Trinity Church, George V Park, Codrington College' where you should turn right.

Along this road on the right-hand side is Holy Trinity Church, rebuilt in 1832 following its destruction in a hurricane. At the T-junction ahead, turn right and follow signs for Thicket which will bring you back to Three Houses Park. Proceed up the hill and at the next junction turn right for Codrington College (see **WHAT TO SEE 3**, **A-Z**) which lies just over a mile along this road. This theological college is set among beautiful grounds and is open to visitors. From here, continue for three quarters of a mile to turn left at the fork signposted 'St. John's Church'. As you climb up the hill there are views of the coastline below, and on reaching the top turn right towards Glebe, where there are direction signs to the church.

33 miles – **St. John's** (see **WHAT TO SEE 3**, **A-Z**) is a church of great historic interest and its elevated position affords a spectacular vista along much of the east coast.

On leaving, go back to the main road to turn right towards Bridgetown, and two miles further on is Four Cross Roads, where you turn right for Villa Nova, which is well signposted.

36 miles – **Villa Nova**. With its fine collection of local antiques, this is one of the best of Barbados's plantation houses (see **WHAT TO SEE 3**, **A-Z**). The house and gardens are open to visitors on weekdays. On exiting, turn left at the end of the drive, proceed through the village of Venture, and after about a mile you will come to a junction. Carry straight over then take first right, down an unmarked and very narrow, rough track which peters out after half a mile. Park at this point, and walk a short distance along the track till you reach a row of three houses. Opposite the last one is a path leading right to the edge of Hackleton's Cliff (see **WHAT TO SEE 3**). There are spectacular views from these heights of over 300 metres.

Return to the junction immediately after Villa Nova, turn left then first right to return to Four Cross Roads, turning right at this junction following the sign 'Gun Hill, Bridgetown'. After 3.8 miles, look out for a sign pointing right to Gun Hill, and follow directions to the top where Gun Hill Signal Station (see **WHAT TO SEE 4**) is located. In the care of the

Sam Lord's Castle

Villa Nova

Codrington College

Barbados National Trust (see **A-Z**), this
beautifully restored building is open
daily. On leaving, turn right towards
Bridgetown, and after a quarter of a mile
turn right at the sign to Francia Plantation
House (see **WHAT TO SEE 4**) which is
reached along a well-signposted road.
The house and grounds, in which there is
a set of original drip stones (see **A-Z**), are
open on weekdays. On leaving Francia,
retrace your steps to the main Bridgetown
road and turn right. At the roundabout at
Haggatt Hall, cross straight over the Errol
Barrow Highway, and proceed down
through the Bridgetown suburbs back
into the city centre.

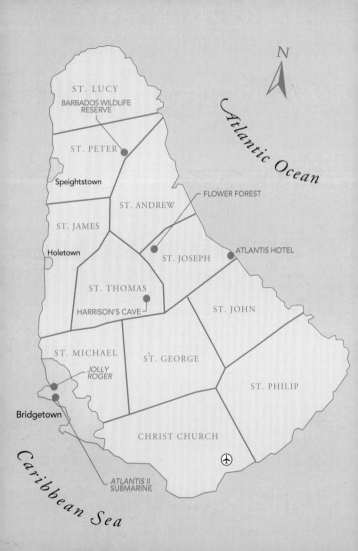

A CRUISE ON THE *JOLLY ROGER* Shallow dock area of deep-water harbour, Bridgetown. ❑ 1000. Evening cruises 1800 Thu., Sat. ❑ Bds $85 (includes transport to and from hotel, buffet meal and drinks except wine and champagne), child 4-12 Bds $45, under 4s free. *An action-packed sail on a 'pirate' ship. Fun for the whole family includes snorkelling over a wreck, walking the plank and rope swinging. See* **A-Z**, **Tours***.*

HARRISON'S CAVE Welchman Hall, St. Thomas. ❑ 0900-1600. ❑ Bds $15, child under 16 Bds $7.50. *Take an electric tram ride into an underground spectacle of caverns, waterfalls, pools, stalactites and stalagmites, all beautifully illuminated. See* EXCURSION 1, **A-Z***.*

FLOWER FOREST Richmond, St. Joseph. ❑ 0900-1700. ❑ Bds $10, child under 16 Bds $5. *A tropical garden in a most picturesque area. A riot of colour mingles with tranquillity, bird song and shy monkeys. See* EXCURSION 1, **A-Z***.*

ATLANTIS II* SUBMARINE TRIP** The Wharf, Bridgetown. ❑ 0900-2000 Mon.-Sat. ❑ Bds $140, child 4-12 Bds $70. No under 4s. *Dive to 150 ft and see colourful fish in surroundings of reefs, sponge gardens, coral formations and a wreck. See* **Tours.*

BARBADOS WILDLIFE RESERVE Farley Hill, St. Peter. ❑ 1000-1700. ❑ Bds $10, child under 12 Bds $5. *Walk along shady paths which wind through four acres of mahogany woods and find exotic animals wandering freely in this fascinating reserve. Look out for monkeys, otters, wallabies and many bird species. See* **A-Z***.*

SUNDAY LUNCH AT ATLANTIS HOTEL Bathsheba, St. Joseph. ❑ 1245-1430 Sun. ❑ Bds $35 inclusive. *Capture the full, evocative flavour of Barbadian cuisine, presented in stunning buffet-style extravagance, at this glorious seaside location. It has offered superb value for over 20 years. See* EXCURSION 1, **Food***.*

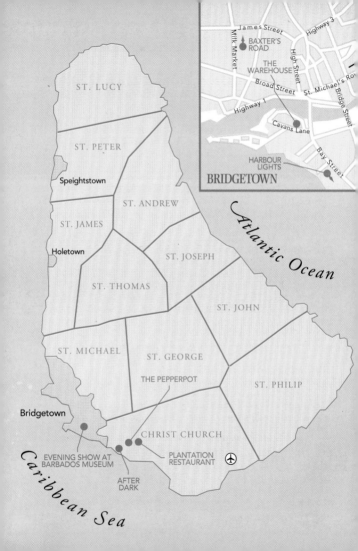

ST. LUCY

ST. PETER

Speightstown

ST. ANDREW

ST. JAMES

Holetown

ST. JOSEPH

ST. THOMAS

ST. JOHN

ST. MICHAEL

ST. GEORGE

ST. PHILIP

THE PEPPERPOT

Bridgetown

CHRIST CHURCH

EVENING SHOW AT
BARBADOS MUSEUM

PLANTATION
RESTAURANT

AFTER
DARK

Atlantic Ocean

Caribbean Sea

James Street

Milk Market

BAXTER'S
ROAD

Highway 3

THE
WAREHOUSE

Broad Street

High Street

St. Michael's Row

Highway 1

Cavans Lane

Bridge Street

HARBOUR
LIGHTS

Bay Street

BRIDGETOWN

EVENING SHOW AT BARBADOS MUSEUM St. Ann's
Garrison, St. Michael. ❑ 1830-2300 Sun., Thu. ❑ $80 Bds.
*A fast-moving, colourful culture show entitled '1627 and All That', by
Barbados' leading dance company. Price includes full buffet dinner,
drinks and tour of museum (see WHAT TO SEE 1, Barbados Museum).*

THE WAREHOUSE Cavans Lane, Bridgetown.
❑ From 2130. ❑ Cover charge.
*One of the island's trendiest discos, featuring the latest sounds and lead-
ing local groups performing live.*

BAXTER'S ROAD Bridgetown.
❑ From 2300.
*Try the Bajan delicacies and drinks on sale at stalls and little restaurants.
Throbbing music adds to the exciting atmosphere. See A-Z, Food.*

AFTER DARK St. Lawrence Gap, Christ Church.
❑ From 2100. ❑ Cover charge.
*Courtyard entertainment includes bands, a disco and floor shows. The
lounge inside, famous for its long bar, has jazz Mon. to Sat. See Music.*

PLANTATION RESTAURANT St. Lawrence Rd, Christ Church.
❑ Dinner shows from 1800 Mon., Fri., Sat. ❑ Bds $80 dinner, show and
drinks; Bds $40 show and drinks only.
*Lively entertainment includes cabaret with limbo, calypso, fire eating,
dancers and steel band, all providing lots of carnival-style atmosphere.*

THE PEPPERPOT St. Lawrence Rd, Christ Church.
❑ From 2100. ❑ Cover charge.
*For over 30 years this has been a popular nightspot with locals and
visitors alike, and a varied programme caters for all ages.*

HARBOUR LIGHTS Marine Villa, Bay St, Bridgetown.
❑ From 2130.
*This open-air, beach-front club, staging a different band each night,
appeals to the younger set.*

N

ST. LUCY

ST. PETER

FARLEY HILL
NATIONAL
PARK

Speightstown

ST. ANDREW

TURNER'S HALL WOODS

ST. JAMES

ANDROMEDA GARDENS

Holetown

ST. JOSEPH

ST. THOMAS

WELCHMAN HALL
GULLY

ST. JOHN

ST. MICHAEL

ST. GEORGE

ST. PHILIP

Bridgetown

CHRIST CHURCH

QUEEN'S
PARK

Atlantic Ocean

Caribbean Sea

PARKS & GARDENS

ANDROMEDA GARDENS Near Bathsheba, St. Joseph.
❏ 0900-1615. ❏ Bds $8, child under 16 Bds $4.
*Created in 1954 and run by the Barbados National Trust (see **A-Z**), this beautiful ten-acre garden sits on high ground overlooking the Atlantic. Paths and bridges meander between trees, ponds, lawns and rich displays of indigenous and foreign shrubs, flowers and ferns. See* **EXCURSION 1**.

TURNER'S HALL WOODS Near Haggatts, St. Andrew.
❏ Daily. ❏ Free.
Although access is very difficult, requiring an arduous walk, these woods form the only remaining area of Barbados' original covering of forest and vegetation. Sturdy footwear should be worn. See **A-Z**.

QUEEN'S PARK Bridgetown.
❏ Daily. ❏ Free.
A short walk from the city, Queen's Park offers a tranquil contrast to the noise and bustle of Bridgetown. The well-maintained gardens contain a lake, a small aviary and many interesting plant, shrub and tree species. Among the park buildings is the impressive Queen's Park House, until 1906 the residence of the general in charge of British troops on the island, and now a theatre and art gallery. See **Arts & Crafts**.

WELCHMAN HALL GULLY Off Highway 2, St. Thomas.
❏ 0900-1700. ❏ Bds $5, child under 12 Bds $2.50.
A one-mile stretch of jungle-like vegetation lying in a natural fissure and containing around 200 plant and tree species, including the bearded fig tree from which Barbados reputedly takes its name ('los barbados' in Portuguese means 'the bearded ones'). Also on view are large stalactites in the gully walls, and you may even spot monkeys darting amongst the tree canopy high above. See **EXCURSION 1**, **Barbados National Trust**.

FARLEY HILL NATIONAL PARK Highway 1, St. Peter.
❏ Daily. ❏ Bds $3.
*Centrepiece of this park is the ruin of Farley Hill (see **A-Z**), one of the island's great plantation mansions. The 17-acre grounds contain species from many countries, and there are superb views towards the east coast.*

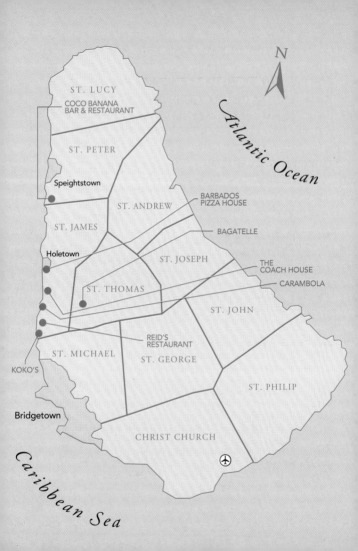

N

ST. LUCY

COCO BANANA
BAR & RESTAURANT

ST. PETER

Atlantic Ocean

Speightstown

ST. ANDREW

BARBADOS
PIZZA HOUSE

ST. JAMES

BAGATELLE

Holetown

ST. JOSEPH

THE
COACH HOUSE

CARAMBOLA

ST. THOMAS

ST. JOHN

REID'S
RESTAURANT

ST. MICHAEL

ST. GEORGE

KOKO'S

ST. PHILIP

Bridgetown

CHRIST CHURCH

Caribbean Sea

CARAMBOLA Derricks, St. James, tel: 432-0832.
❑ 1830-2230 Mon.-Sat. ❑ Expensive.
Set on a cliff overlooking the Caribbean, this restaurant enjoys one of the most romantic settings on the island. Superbly prepared French cuisine is backed by an interesting wine list and attentive service.

BAGATELLE Off Highway 2a, St. Thomas, tel: 421-6767.
❑ 1900-2230 Mon.-Sat. ❑ Expensive.
This superior restaurant at Bagatelle Great House is famous for food, service and ambience. The fairy-tale setting makes dining here a pleasure.

REID'S RESTAURANT Highway 1, St. James, tel: 432-7623.
❑ 1800-2230 Mon.-Sat. ❑ Moderate-Expensive.
The dining area of this acclaimed restaurant is in the covered garden of a beautiful 18thC house. Lobster and other seafood is a speciality, though the imaginative menu also includes pork, poultry and beef dishes.

COCO BANANA BAR & RESTAURANT Road View, St. Peter,
tel: 422-0640. ❑ 1900-0100 Tue.-Sat. ❑ Moderate.
This good-value restaurant enjoys an informal atmosphere. The menu describes dishes in a light-hearted fashion but food is genuinely good.

KOKO'S Prospect, St. James, tel: 424-4557.
❑ 1830-2230. ❑ Inexpensive-Moderate.
*The emphasis at this pleasant beachside restaurant is on local food cooked Bajan style, full of deliciously tasty spices and sauces (see **Food**).*

BARBADOS PIZZA HOUSE Holetown, St. James, tel: 432-0227.
❑ 1000-2300 Mon.-Thu., 1000-2400 Fri.-Sun. ❑ Inexpensive.
For the budget conscious, this establishment offers a splendid range of pizza, pasta, fish, vegetarian and salad dishes. Full bar service available.

THE COACH HOUSE Paynes Bay, St. James, tel: 432-1163.
❑ 1200-1445, 1800-0200. Lunches Sun.-Fri. only. ❑ Inexpensive.
A lively English-style pub and restaurant. In the evenings you can eat in the dining room or choose from the bar menu. Live music most nights.

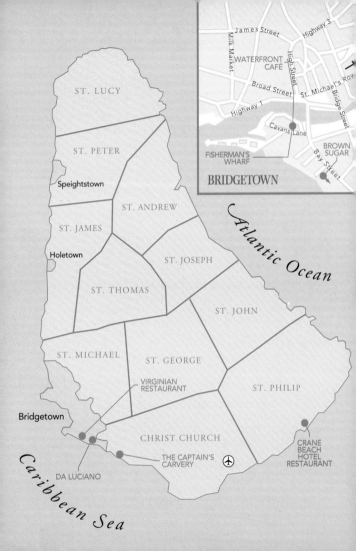

ST. LUCY

ST. PETER

Speightstown

ST. ANDREW

ST. JAMES

Holetown

ST. JOSEPH

ST. THOMAS

ST. JOHN

ST. MICHAEL

ST. GEORGE

Bridgetown

VIRGINIAN
RESTAURANT

ST. PHILIP

CHRIST CHURCH

CRANE
BEACH
HOTEL
RESTAURANT

THE CAPTAIN'S
CARVERY

DA LUCIANO

Atlantic Ocean

Caribbean Sea

JAMES STREET

Milk Market

WATERFRONT
CAFÉ

Highway 3

High Street

Broad Street

St. Michael's Row

Bridge Street

Highway 1

Cavans Lane

FISHERMAN'S
WHARF

BROWN
SUGAR

Bay Street

BRIDGETOWN

DA LUCIANO 'Staten', Hastings, Christ Church, tel: 427-5518.
❏ 1830-2200. ❏ Expensive.
Set in a tastefully converted late-19thC Great House, this restaurant provides a perfect blend of fine Italian cuisine and elegant, romantic dining.

VIRGINIAN RESTAURANT Seaview Hotel, Hastings, Christ Church, tel: 427-7963. ❏ 1800-2300. ❏ Moderate-Expensive.
Housed in an 18thC building, this upstairs restaurant has classic decor and antique furnishings. House speciality is steak, and lobster in season.

CRANE BEACH HOTEL RESTAURANT The Crane, St. Philip, tel: 423-6220. ❏ 1200-1500, 1900-2230. ❏ Moderate.
This award-winning restaurant serves Crane chub and lobster freshly caught from nearby reefs. In a spectacular setting atop Atlantic cliffs.

BROWN SUGAR Aquatic Gap, St. Michael, tel: 426-7684.
❏ 1130-1430 Mon.-Fri., 1800-2200 Mon.-Sat. ❏ Inexpensive-Moderate.
*Fine Caribbean cuisine (see **Food**) features at this popular restaurant. The 'Planters Buffet' lunch offers exceptional value at around Bds $25.*

FISHERMAN'S WHARF Careenage, Bridgetown, tel: 436-7778.
❏ 1130-2200 Mon.-Fri., 1830-2200 Sat., 1130-1500 Sun.
❏ Inexpensive-Moderate.
*Upstairs restaurant offering local specialities, with seafood, and a Bajan lunch (see **Food**) on Fri. and Sun. Chicken, pork and steak also feature.*

WATERFRONT CAFÉ Careenage, Bridgetown, tel: 427-0093.
❏ 1000-2200 Mon.-Sat. ❏ Inexpensive.
*Snacks, salads, fish dishes and grills are served cheerfully in a delightful waterside setting. Be early for lunch as this is a popular venue. Evening entertainment includes jazz, folk and piano music (see **Music**).*

THE CAPTAIN'S CARVERY The Ship Inn, St. Lawrence Gap, Christ Church, tel: 435-6961. ❏ 1200-1500 Sun.-Fri., 1830-2230 daily.
❏ Inexpensive.
Dinners and buffet lunches feature a fine selection of roasts and salads.

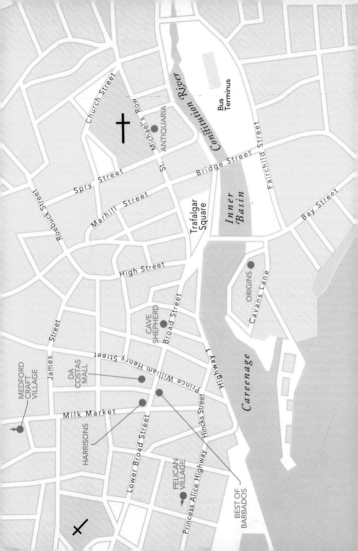

SHOPPING 1

❏ See **Opening Times**.

HARRISONS Nos 1 & 37 Broad St, Bridgetown.
A comprehensive range of crystal, china, figurines, jewellery, perfume, leather goods and ceramics on sale at No. 1, with tobacco, spirits and some local items at No. 37. Most goods can be bought duty-free.

DA COSTAS MALL Broad St, Bridgetown.
Pleasant, air-conditioned, two-storey arcade of assorted shops selling a wide range of goods including cameras, jewellery, local crafts, clothing, beach wear, crystal and china.

ANTIQUARIA St. Michael's Row, Bridgetown.
Interesting range of fine local antique furniture, early maps, silver, brass-ware, china and antique jewellery on sale. Overseas shipping available.

MEDFORD CRAFT VILLAGE Lower Barbarees Hill, Bridgetown.
Locally produced handicrafts and souvenirs available, with an opportunity to see craftsmen at work on site.

CAVE SHEPHERD Broad St, Bridgetown.
Barbados' largest department store, offering a vast range of goods, including duty-free items.

ORIGINS Careenage, Bridgetown.
An upmarket boutique selling classic garments in natural fibres, clothing accessories and artwork.

BEST OF BARBADOS Mall 34, Broad St, Bridgetown; & branches.
*Everything sold here is made or designed in Barbados, from high-quality tableware and clothes to Jill Walker's fine prints (see **Best Buys**).*

PELICAN VILLAGE Princess Alice Highway, Bridgetown.
*Three-acre complex of shops selling a huge variety of locally made arts and crafts, including straw craft, pottery, leather goods, shell and coral ornaments, wood carvings, batik and paintings (see **Best Buys**).*

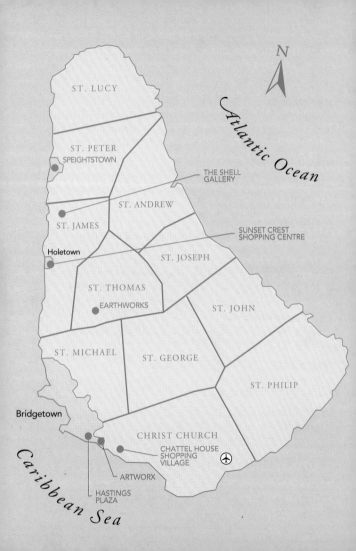

N

ST. LUCY

ST. PETER
SPEIGHTSTOWN

THE SHELL
GALLERY

ST. ANDREW

ST. JAMES

SUNSET CREST
SHOPPING CENTRE

Holetown

ST. JOSEPH

ST. THOMAS
EARTHWORKS

ST. JOHN

ST. MICHAEL

ST. GEORGE

ST. PHILIP

Bridgetown

CHRIST CHURCH

CHATTEL HOUSE
SHOPPING
VILLAGE

ARTWORX

HASTINGS
PLAZA

Atlantic Ocean

Caribbean Sea

❏ See **Opening Times** where no other times are given.

EARTHWORKS Shop Hill, St. Thomas.
❏ 0900-1700 Mon.-Fri., 0900-1300 Sat.
*Uniquely designed earthenware, all created on the premises from good-quality local clay (see **Best Buys**). See the potters at work.*

THE SHELL GALLERY Carlton House, St. James.
❏ 0900-1600 Mon.-Fri., or tel: 422-2635 for alternative arrangements.
An interesting range of shell- or coral-related items for sale. Shell mirrors are a speciality. Made-to-order service available.

HASTINGS PLAZA Highway 7, Hastings, Christ Church.
This small, neatly styled plaza embraces a bank, boutiques, and shops selling beachwear fashion, books, jewellery, souvenirs and local crafts.

ARTWORX Quayside Centre, Rockley, Christ Church.
❏ 0900-1800 Mon.-Sat.
Gallery shop selling original paintings, sculptures, prints and fabrics, as well as pottery and jewellery, all from local artists and craftspeople.

CHATTEL HOUSE SHOPPING VILLAGE St. Lawrence Gap, Christ Church.
*Courtyard setting with colourful chattel-house style (see **A-Z**) shops selling beachwear, surfing equipment, crafts, fashions, wines and spirits, and souvenirs. There's an ice-cream parlour and a hair salon too.*

SUNSET CREST SHOPPING CENTRE Holetown, St. James.
A large complex of shops selling a wide selection of goods and services, including a bank, supermarket and restaurant.

SPEIGHTSTOWN St. Peter.
*Barbados' most northerly town is well served with banks, a post office, supermarket, a good variety of shops, chemists, and a branch of Cave Shepherd's (see **SHOPPING 1**) department store where many items can be purchased duty-free. See **Speightstown**.*

BOAT TRIPS

Glass-bottom boats offer a relaxed way of observing the numerous and colourful marine species which frequent inshore coral reefs. Trips are available from several hotel locations; ❏ *c.Bds $12, child Bds $8. Four-hour 'party cruises' on the Mississippi-style* Bajan Queen *leave Bridgetown's deep-water harbour;* ❏ *Tue., Thu.-Sat.* ❏ *Bds $85, child Bds $45 including buffet, drinks and entertainment. See* **Water Sports**. *The pirate ship* Jolly Roger *sails daily from the harbour (see* **MUSTS**).*

SAILING CRUISES

*For minimum parties of around six people, go to the Careenage in Bridgetown where yachts can be chartered complete with skipper and crew for half- or full-day cruises. A choice of catamarans (*Tiami, Wind Warrior, Irish Mist II*) or monohulls (*Limbo Lady, Secret Love*) will take you on a four- or five-hour lunch cruise.* ❏ *c.Bds $100 per person including food and drinks. Advance bookings are advisable. Sunset, moonlight and overnight cruises are also available. See* **Water Sports**.

DEEP SEA FISHING

Kingfish, marlin, barracuda, dorado and sail fish can all be caught in the seas off Barbados. Up to six people can hire a skippered, fully equipped boat. ❏ *c.Bds $500 per boat per half day including drinks and snacks.*

SUBMARINE TRIP

The trip of a lifetime, the submarine Atlantis II *takes you to depths of 150 ft by day or night. See* **MUSTS**.

SAILING

Small catamarans and sunfish dinghies can be hired from operators along the west and south coasts. ❏ *c.Bds $25-40 per hr, depending on size of craft. See* **Water Sports**.

JET SKIING

These marine machines give an exhilarating experience as you race over the waves. Hire from Jet Ski Rentals in Holetown, tel: 432-1340, or from selected water-sports centres on the west coast. ❏ *c.Bds $35 for 20 min.*

SPORTS & ACTIVITIES 2

SNORKELLING
Good near the west- and south-coast reefs where there is lots of marine life to observe. ❏ c.Bds $18 to hire a mask, snorkel and fins. Snorkellers should use a brightly coloured float to warn boats of their presence.

SCUBA DIVING
Barbados is a great place for the novice or experienced diver, with reefs and wrecks to explore by day or night, depending on your level of experience. Diving courses are run by: Shades of Blue at Coral Reef Club, tel: 422-3215; Dive Boat Safari at Hilton Beach, tel: 427-4350; Exploresub Barbados in St. Lawrence Gap, tel: 435-6542, and several others (see the yellow-pages section of the telephone directory). ❏ c.Bds $100 for beginners' courses with instructors including equipment hire. ❏ c.Bds $85 per trip for those with the necessary certificate. See **Water Sports**.

WINDSURFING
Barbados is said to offer the best windsurfing in the Caribbean, and with the contrast between the calmer west and breezier south coasts, both beginners and the experienced will find conditions to suit their needs. Novices are probably best to take lessons at a west-coast centre before progressing to the more challenging areas around Maxwell Beach in the south. The seas off Silver Sands Hotel, round from South Point, should only be tackled by the very experienced. Equipment can be hired from: Willie's Water Sports at Paradise Beach, tel: 424-0888, or Heywoods Resort, tel: 422-4900; Windsurfing Club at Maxwell, tel: 428-7277; and Silver Sands Hotel, tel: 428-6001. Lessons available. See **Water Sports**.

SURFING
Bathsheba on the east coast is where the serious surfers congregate and championships are held there occasionally. Also popular is the Crane area on the southeast coast, and near Oistins when conditions permit.

PARASAILING
A thrilling way to sightsee as you float beneath a parachute towed by a speedboat way below. Operators tend to be found mainly around the west coast. ❏ c.Bds $50 per ten-min 'flight'. See **Water Sports**.

WALKING

*The Barbados National Trust (see **A-Z**) organises weekly guided walks to suit all categories, tel: 426-2421 for details and itineraries. See **Walks**.*

HORSERIDING

A great way to take in the beautiful scenery, and your guide ensures you don't get lost. Trail rides are available from: Brighton Stables, Black Rock, tel: 425-9381; Caribbean International Riding Centre, Christ Church, tel: 423-0186; Wilcox Riding Stables, Christ Church, tel: 428-3610; and Tony's Riding School, St. Peter, tel: 422-1549. ❏ c.Bds $50 per hr.

CYCLING

*Roads are narrow and often rough so take care at all times, though motorists tend to be sympathetic to cyclists. Fun Seekers Inc., Christ Church, tel: 435-8206, and M.A. Williams, Hastings, tel: 427-3955, both hire bikes. ❏ c.Bds $15-20 per day. See **Bicycle & Motorcycle Hire**.*

GOLF

There is one 18-hole course at Sandy Lane, St. James, tel: 432-1145; ❏ Bds $60 per round. Heywoods Resort, St. Peter, tel: 422-4900, and Rockley Resort, Christ Church, tel: 435-7880, each have a nine-hole course;❏ c.Bds $30 per round. c.Bds $40 for club hire for 18 holes, available at all three courses. Advance tee reservations are advised.

TENNIS

Very popular, so book courts in advance. There are courts at: Sunset Crest Beach Club, St. James, tel: 432-1309; Sandy Lane Hotel, St. James, tel: 432-1311; Heywoods Resort, St. Peter, tel: 422-4900; Rockley Resort, Christ Church, tel: 435-7880; Paradise Beach Club, St. James, tel: 424-0888; Casuarina Beach Club, Dover, Christ Church, tel: 428-3600. ❏ c.Bds $15-25 per court per hr. ❏ c.Bds $10 per hr for racquet hire.

SQUASH

Air-conditioned courts are located at Heywoods Resort, St. Peter, tel: 422-4900; Rockley Resort, Christ Church, tel: 435-7880; Sea View Hotel, Hastings, tel: 426-1450. ❏ c.Bds $20 per court per hr.

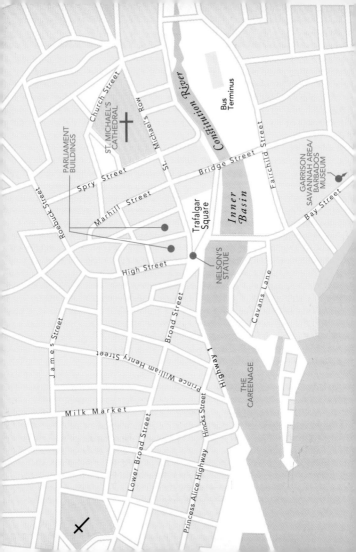

BARBADOS MUSEUM St. Ann's Garrison, Bridgetown.
❏ 1000-1800 Mon.-Sat. ❏ Bds $4, child Bds $1.
Housed in the precincts of the old military prison, the museum's exhibits include natural history, the arts, archaeology and Barbadian history as well as a rare collection of antique maps and prints. A courtyard café and a shop are on the premises. See **A-Z**.

NELSON'S STATUE Trafalgar Square, Bridgetown.
Erected in 1813 long before its counterpart in London, it is puzzling that whilst he is correctly depicted as having lost his right arm, his right eye appears perfectly normal despite losing it fully two years before his limb! See **Nelson**.

ST. MICHAEL'S CATHEDRAL St. Michael's Row, Bridgetown.
One of the three oldest surviving churches in Barbados, rebuilt following its destruction in the hurricane of 1780. The first church built on this site was constructed between 1660 and 1665. See **Churches**, **A-Z**.

PARLIAMENT BUILDINGS Trafalgar Sq., Bridgetown.
These Gothic-style buildings, constructed in the 1870s, accommodate the House of Assembly and some government offices. When Parliament is in session debates can be observed from the public gallery.

THE CAREENAGE Bridgetown.
Now a tranquil inner basin lined with cafés and shops with plush yachts moored alongside, this area was once Barbados' main port where vessels would unload their cargo for storage in surrounding warehouses. The name comes from the word 'careening', which is the method of cleaning or repairing the hull of a boat by keeling it over to one side.

GARRISON SAVANNAH AREA Highway 7, 1.5 miles west of Bridgetown.
This area formed the headquarters of the British military presence in the eastern Caribbean until 1905 when troops were withdrawn. Most of the buildings and artefacts to be seen reflect this connection. See EXCURSION 2, **A-Z**.

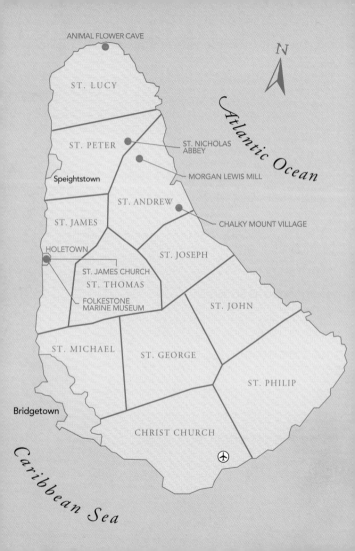

ANIMAL FLOWER CAVE

ST. LUCY

N

ST. PETER

ST. NICHOLAS ABBEY

MORGAN LEWIS MILL

Speightstown

ST. ANDREW

ST. JAMES

CHALKY MOUNT VILLAGE

HOLETOWN

ST. JOSEPH

ST. JAMES CHURCH

ST. THOMAS

FOLKESTONE MARINE MUSEUM

ST. JOHN

ST. MICHAEL

ST. GEORGE

ST. PHILIP

Bridgetown

CHRIST CHURCH

Atlantic Ocean

Caribbean Sea

ANIMAL FLOWER CAVE St. Lucy.
❏ Daily. ❏ Bds $3, child Bds $1.50.
Descend by deep staircase into a series of caves containing lots of colourful sea anemones. Dramatically located at the island's northern point where 12-ft waves pound the cliffs. See EXCURSION 1, A-Z.

ST. NICHOLAS ABBEY St. Peter.
❏ 1000-1530 Mon.-Fri. ❏ Bds $5.
A fine Jacobean plantation house built c.1650. Nearby is Cherry Tree Hill which affords lovely views of the east coast. See EXCURSION 1, A-Z.

CHALKY MOUNT VILLAGE St. Andrew.
This is the centre of 'The Potteries' and local residents working in wooden houses perched on the sides of elevated steep hills produce and sell good-quality earthenware (see Best Buys). See EXCURSION 1.

MORGAN LEWIS MILL St. Andrew.
❏ 0900-1700 Mon.-Sat. ❏ Bds $2, child Bds $1.
The last-remaining complete windmill in the Caribbean. The museum inside portrays the history of the sugar mills. See EXCURSION 1.

HOLETOWN St. James.
A popular tourist area with shops, restaurants and fine beaches nearby, this is where the first settlers landed in 1627, though the commemorative memorial bears the wrong date! See EXCURSION 1, A-Z.

ST. JAMES CHURCH Holetown, St. James.
It is believed a wooden church was erected here in 1629, and the present building contains parts of a stone construction from around 1680. See the original church bell of 1696, and font of 1684. See EXCURSION 1, A-Z.

FOLKESTONE MARINE MUSEUM Holetown, St. James.
❏ Sun.-Fri. ❏ Bds $1.
Various corals, shells, sponges, skeletons and antiquities from wrecks on display, as well as an aquarium. Glass-bottom-boat trips and snorkelling can be had from the adjacent beach. See EXCURSION 1.

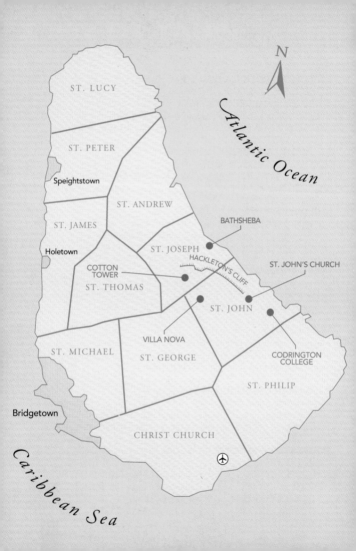

N

ST. LUCY

ST. PETER

Speightstown

ST. ANDREW

ST. JAMES

Holetown

BATHSHEBA

ST. JOSEPH

HACKLETON'S CLIFF

COTTON
TOWER

ST. JOHN'S CHURCH

ST. THOMAS

ST. JOHN

VILLA NOVA

ST. MICHAEL

ST. GEORGE

CODRINGTON
COLLEGE

ST. PHILIP

Bridgetown

CHRIST CHURCH

Atlantic Ocean

Caribbean Sea

COTTON TOWER St. Joseph.
*Under the care of the Barbados National Trust (see **A-Z**), this 19thC signal station has been restored. The only other remaining of the original six is at Gun Hill (see **WHAT TO SEE 4**). See **EXCURSION 1**, **Signal Stations**.*

BATHSHEBA St. Joseph.
*A picturesque area which has escaped the ravages of tourist development, and, in contrast to the calm west coast, the seas at this fishing village produce large waves, making it a popular venue for surfers. See **SPORTS & ACTIVITIES 2**, **Water Sports**.*

HACKLETON'S CLIFF St. John.
*The top of this impressive geographical feature can be reached by a rough, narrow track. The cliff affords spectacular views extending over a vast area of the east coast. See **EXCURSION 2**.*

ST. JOHN'S CHURCH St. John.
*Situated on an elevated position, this church contains an ornately carved pulpit, a Westmacott sculpture, floor tablets dating from the mid 1600s, and the tomb of 17thC plantation owner Ferdinand Paleologus. See **EXCURSION 2**, **A-Z**.*

CODRINGTON COLLEGE St. John.
*Set in peaceful surroundings with a lake and palm-tree-lined drive, this historic Anglican theological college contains some interesting architecture. See **EXCURSION 2**, **A-Z**.*

VILLA NOVA St. John.
❏ 0900-1600 Mon.-Fri. ❏ Bds $6.
*Built in 1834, this plantation house was owned from 1965-71 by the late Earl of Avon, Sir Anthony Eden, the former British Prime Minister. See **EXCURSION 2**, **A-Z**.*

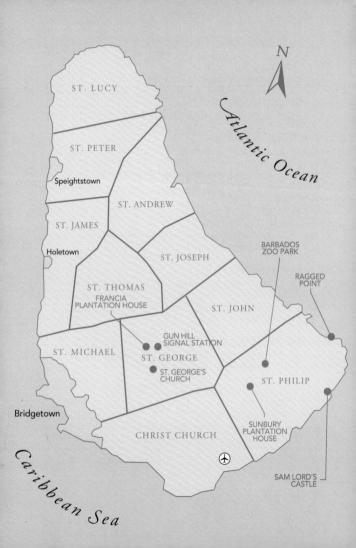

N

Atlantic Ocean

ST. LUCY

ST. PETER

Speightstown

ST. ANDREW

ST. JAMES

Holetown

ST. JOSEPH

BARBADOS
ZOO PARK

RAGGED
POINT

ST. THOMAS

FRANCIA
PLANTATION HOUSE

ST. JOHN

GUN HILL
SIGNAL STATION

ST. MICHAEL

ST. GEORGE

ST. GEORGE'S
CHURCH

ST. PHILIP

Bridgetown

CHRIST CHURCH

SUNBURY
PLANTATION
HOUSE

SAM LORD'S
CASTLE

Caribbean Sea

SAM LORD'S CASTLE St. Philip.
This splendid Regency mansion was the 19thC home of the celebrated malefactor Sam Lord. Now a lavish resort hotel. See EXCURSION 2, **A-Z**.

SUNBURY PLANTATION HOUSE St. Philip.
❏ 1000-1600. ❏ Bds $8, child under 12 Bds $4.
Filled with antique furniture, prints, maps and a horse-drawn-carriage collection, this fine 300-year-old mansion evokes an atmosphere of stylish life on a sugar estate in the 18th-19thC. See EXCURSION 2, **A-Z**.

RAGGED POINT St. Philip.
Splendid views of Atlantic breakers can be had along this rugged bit of coastline. See EXCURSION 2.

BARBADOS ZOO PARK Oughterson House, St. Philip.
❏ 1000-1700, Mon.-Sat., 1100-1700 Sun. ❏ Bds $8, child Bds $4.
See a variety of birds, animals and reptiles, as well as tropical tree and plant species, in the grounds of this single-storey 18thC plantation house which has some interesting West Indian antiques. See EXCURSION 2.

FRANCIA PLANTATION HOUSE St. George.
❏ 1000-1600 Mon.-Fri. ❏ Bds $6, child Bds $3.
Terraced lawns and well-maintained gardens grace this elegant private house of French and Barbadian architectural styles. It contains a fine collection of antique furniture, maps and prints. A complete set of original drip stones (see **A-Z***) can be seen in the courtyard. See* EXCURSION 2.

GUN HILL SIGNAL STATION St. George.
❏ 0900-1700. ❏ Bds $5.
Fully restored by Barbados National Trust (see **A-Z***), it affords great views over the west and south of the island. See* EXCURSION 2, **Signal Stations**.

ST. GEORGE'S CHURCH St. George.
One of only three island churches to survive the 1831 hurricane. Benjamin West's painting The Resurrection *hangs over the altar. See* **Churches, A-Z**.

Accidents & Breakdowns: If you are involved in a road accident, take the other driver's name, address, telephone number and vehicle registration number, and call the police (see **A-Z**) immediately. They will ensure that all necessary details are properly recorded, and their presence is strongly advised in case any legal proceedings ensue. If damage to a hired vehicle has occurred contact your car rental company and advise them of the situation so that they can arrange for breakdown services to attend if required. Do not attempt to make your own arrangements direct with a garage for repairs as rental companies have their own facilities and you may find you have breached your hire contract by doing so. See **Consulates**, **Driving**, **Emergency Numbers**.

Accommodation: Types of accommodation range from large international hotels through smaller hotels to guesthouses, self-catering apartments and privately rented villas. The Barbados Board of Tourism's inspectors constantly visit establishments (though not private ones) and a list of rates published by the Board each season is available from their offices. There is no formal rating system. The peak winter season runs from mid December to mid April and advance booking is essential, though the slightly cheaper summer season (the rest of the year) is also popular, and advanced booking is recommended. See **Tourist Information**.

Airport: Barbados is served by Grantley Adams International Airport, the largest and most modern in the region. Located in the southeast of the island, approximately 11 miles from the capital, Bridgetown, it handles regular flights to and from the UK, USA and Canada, as well as Caribbean destinations. Operators include British Airways, BWIA (British West Indian Airways) and Pan Am. Airport taxis (see **A-Z**) serve all island destinations, and some larger hotels operate their own direct minibus services. Taxis are not metered and typical fares from the airport vary from Bds $12 for a short journey, to Bds $50 if travelling to the north of the island. The fare to Bridgetown is around Bds $26 (see **Tipping**). Red-cap porters operate in the baggage-reclaim area, with Bds $1 per bag being the usual charge. On leaving Barbados you will

be subject to a departure tax of Bds $25, payable at the airport.
Flight information:

British Airways   tel: 428-1660
BWIA   tel: 428-1650
Pan Am   tel: 428-1660

Animal Flower Cave: Situated at the most northerly point of the
island, this sea-formed cave with three caverns containing sea
anemones (known as animal flowers) and colourful algae is open daily,
and guided tours are available. The scenery in this area is spectacular,
with huge waves pounding the cliffs and rocks. See **EXCURSION 1, WHAT
TO SEE 2**.

Architecture: Despite the ravages of hurricanes over the centuries,
fine examples of Barbados's architectural heritage remain to this day.
From chattel houses (see **A-Z**) to plantation houses, and churches to
Jacobean mansions, many interesting buildings can be visited. The
influence of Georgian architecture is particularly noticeable. The Barbados National Trust (see **A-Z**) places plaques on buildings of special
note, and they are always pleased to provide information on request.

Chattel House

Arts & Crafts: A diversity of handicrafts can be found in Barbados, and work by local artists can be seen in galleries such as Queen's Park House (see **PARKS & GARDENS**) and shops. Pottery, batik, straw craft, jewellery, leather craft, woodcarving, shell and coral craft are widely available and materials used include bark, fish scales, jute, khuskhus grass, coconut shells, leaves and mahogany. See **SHOPPING**, **Best Buys**.

Baby-Sitters: There are no baby-sitting agencies but most hotels will provide this service. Individuals offering to baby-sit occasionally advertise in *The Barbados Advocate* or *The Nation* daily newspapers (see **A-Z**), and the cost is around $10 per hour. See **Children**.

Banks: See **Currency**, **Money**, **Opening Times**.

Barbados Museum: This Bridgetown museum is an excellent place to discover more about the island in unintimidating and pleasant surroundings. Carefully restored buildings (once part of the Garrison's prison) contain galleries of natural and local history, maps, furniture, prints, paintings, decorative arts and other items. The show '1627 And All That' (see **NIGHTLIFE**) is performed here twice a week and admission includes a tour of the museum. In addition to a shop there is also a café offering morning coffee, light lunches and afternoon teas (see **WHAT TO SEE 1**).

Barbados National Trust: The Trust owns and operates five properties: Morgan Lewis Mill (see **WHAT TO SEE 2**), Welchman Hall Gully (see **PARKS & GARDENS**), Sir Frank Hutson Sugar Machinery Museum, Gun Hill Signal Station (see **WHAT TO SEE 4**), and Andromeda Tropical Gardens (see **PARKS & GARDENS**). Members of the National Trust in Britain are admitted free to these properties on production of their membership card, but it is advisable to first make contact with the Trust's headquarters at Ronald Tree House, 10th Avenue, Belville, Bridgetown, tel: 436-9033 in case a special pass is required. Though not open to the public, the Trust also owns Cotton Tower Signal Station (see **Signal Stations**). Restoration projects in hand include the Synagogue and Cemetery. The Trust organises the annual Open House programme (see **A-Z**) and a series of Sunday walks (see **SPORTS & ACTIVITIES 3**, **Walks**).

Barbados Wildlife Reserve: This reserve is primarily a monkey sanctuary offering visitors a unique opportunity to see them and a number of other animals, including otters and wallabies, as well as birds and reptiles, at close range in mainly uncaged surroundings. Paths, shaded by lush tropical vegetation and mahogany trees, lead you through four acres of grounds. Don't forget your camera. See **MUSTS**.

Baxter's Road: Also called 'The Street That Never Sleeps', Baxter's Road is located in the New Orleans district of Bridgetown. A popular venue for locals and visitors alike, it is an exciting place to experience after 2300. A huge variety of hot or cold local delicacies and drinks is available from vendors' stalls, small restaurants or bars. Try the succulent chicken, fish or pork dishes and enjoy the music which plays on until almost dawn. See **NIGHTLIFE**, **Food**.

Beaches: All beaches are open to the public, though several of the
best are fronted by hotels, particularly on the west and south coasts.
Provided you intend using a hotel's facilities (for example, the bar or
restaurant) you should have little difficulty in gaining access to beaches
adjoining its premises. Deckchairs or sunloungers at these locations are
not usually for use by the public. Otherwise, access points are normally
found between beachfront properties, and NCC (National Conservation
Commission) signs – red lettering on a white background – also point to
relevant routes. Seas off the west-coast beaches are mostly calm, and
the south-coast seas are slightly rougher but the east coast constantly
receives turbulent Atlantic rollers, making bathing ill-advised and often
dangerous because of strong currents and tidal flows. Lifeguard stations
(see **A–Z**) are positioned on most main beaches around the island. All
beaches consist of fine, white-coral sand and are generally clean of
debris and seaweed. Sea urchins (see **A–Z**) can occasionally be seen
lying on the sand and their needles inflict a painful jab if trodden upon.
As Barbados lies within a tropical region and the sun's rays are intense,

swimming and sunbathing should be limited during the first few days of your visit (see **Sunbathing**). Many beaches are tree-lined and thus offer some shade. Topless or nude bathing is not allowed. Vendors selling local crafts, dresses, sun hats, fruit, baskets, etc. operate on most beaches, and they are usually prepared to bargain over prices (see **Best Buys**). Note that the beaches which are recommended in BEACHES 3 are on a stretch of coastline facing the North Atlantic, and very strong tidal currents and undertows are prevalent along its entire length. Though often spectacular, the large waves crashing on to beaches and rocks can be dangerous even for the strongest and most experienced swimmer. Heed local advice at all times, and never bathe alone.
See BEACHES.

Best Buys: Most stores in Bridgetown and a number of the smaller shops on the west and south coasts sell a range of duty-free goods. These particular items are identified by dual-priced labels showing both the local price and the duty-free price available for visitors, and to take advantage of this facility you must produce your passport and return travel ticket. You can purchase and take away for immediate use a variety of goods including cameras, jewellery, clothing, binoculars and

watches. Other goods such as tobacco, alcohol and electrical items can also be bought duty-free and they will be delivered to the airport for collection as you leave Barbados. Remember that restrictions on duty-free imports will apply on your return home (see **Passports & Customs**).
Local handicrafts are on sale throughout the island: in Bridgetown's Pelican Village (see SHOPPING 1) a comprehensive range of goods is available. Best Of Barbados shops, at several locations, also carry a good selection (see SHOPPING 1). Locally crafted items (see **Arts & Crafts**) include coral jewellery, leather work, shell ornaments, wooden carvings and batik prints, as well as hats,

bags, baskets and mats all made from straw. Local clay-pottery craft can be found in shops around the island, or direct from the potteries at Chalky Mount (see **WHAT TO SEE 2**) or at Earthworks (see **SHOPPING 2**). When you are on the beach, it's unlikely that you will miss the attentions of vendors plying for trade. Some reasonable bargains can be obtained by negotiating for discounts (it's best to pay in local dollars) and merchandise on offer usually includes straw goods, coral craft, cotton dresses and fabrics, jewellery and general souvenirs. See **SHOPPING**, **Markets**, **Shopping**.

Bicycle & Motorcycle Hire: Bicycle hire (see **SPORTS & ACTIVITIES 3**) costs between Bds $15 and Bds $20 per day, or Bds $12 per day for three days' hire. Weekly rates start at Bds $60. To rent a motorcycle (70-90cc only are available) you must be 21 years old and possess a valid driving licence. Single seaters are known as 'mopeds' and two seaters are called 'scooters'. Rental charges are around Bds $60 per day, or Bds $300 per week for a two seater, and Bds $32 per day, or Bds $155 per week for a single seater. Rates include insurance cover and helmet hire. Bicycles and scooters can be hired from Fun Seekers Inc., Rockley Main Rd, Christ Church, tel: 435-8206. See **Driving**.

Bridgetown: Pop: 80,000. Bridgetown, founded in 1628, is the island's largest city as well as its capital and principal commercial centre. It is a lively place, divided by a random maze of bustling, narrow streets and by the Constitution River which connects to the sea through the Careenage at the southern end of the city, where pavement cafés and moored yachts harmonise in a Mediterranean-style atmosphere. From large stores in the main street (Broad St) selling goods from all over the world, to wayside stalls and the markets at Fairchild St and Cheapside, a vast array of goods is on display, and interesting articles such as antiques and local fashions can be found in side-street shops. Many historical buildings are open to view and places of interest include Nelson's Column (see **Nelson**), Trafalgar Square, House of Assembly, St. Michael's Cathedral (see **A-Z**), and, just out of the centre, the Garrison Savannah area (see **A-Z**) and the Barbados Museum (see **A-Z**). A good variety of eating places will be found offering everything

from local delicacies to international dishes, and Baxter's Road (see **A-Z**) at night shouldn't be missed. See **NIGHTLIFE**, **RESTAURANTS 2**, **SHOPPING 1**, **WHAT TO SEE 1**.

Budget:

Hotel breakfast	Bds $10-30
Lunch	Bds $15-40
Flying fish sandwich	Bds $12
Dish of the day	Bds $15-20
Tea	Bds $2-4 per cup
Coffee	Bds $2-4 per cup
House wine	Bds $6 per glass; from Bds $35 per carafe
Beer	Bds $3-6
Cinema ticket	Bds $8
Museum ticket (Barbados Museum)	Bds $4
Bus ticket	Bds $1 per journey

Buses: Buses connect all parts of the island and no matter how far you travel the fare is always $1 Bds per trip, so this method of transport

is excellent value. There are two systems: government buses (coloured blue with yellow flashes) and private buses (coloured yellow with blue trims), and both charge the same, though only the private operators will give you change. For destinations to the north and along the west coast from Bridgetown the government bus terminals are at Lower Green and Princess Alice Highway. Use the Fairchild St terminal for south and east destinations. There is also a terminal at Speightstown which services the northern areas and direct routes to Bathsheba and Oistins also operate from there. The latter service is known as the 'bypass bus' because it misses out Bridgetown altogether. Private buses operate from Temple Yard, Probyn St, and River Rd in Bridgetown.

Destinations are shown above the windscreen on government buses, and on the bottom left corner of the windscreen on private buses. Bus stops are marked either 'To City' or 'Out of City', the city being Bridgetown, so it is easy to identify your direction of travel, but do remember to put your hand out to stop the bus. See **Tours**, **Transport**.

Cameras & Photography: Shops and stores selling film will be found in most areas, and major brands are widely obtainable. A 36-exposure film costs around $20 Bds for prints, and $27.50 Bds for transparencies. Developing-and-printing services are available though prices are rather high – around $30 Bds for 36 mounted transparencies, and $40 Bds for 36 prints. One-day developing services are also available. When taking your camera outdoors directly from an air-conditioned room or car, it is possible that some misting may occur on the lens owing to the sudden temperature variation and picture quality may be affected, so allow a few moments for condensation to clear. On your departure remove any undeveloped films and your camera from hand luggage before it is put through the x-ray machine at the airport.

Careenage, The: See WHAT TO SEE 1.

Car Hire: Car hire is extremely popular among visitors, and is very convenient for exploring, touring and sightseeing at your own pace. Because of this it is advisable during particularly busy periods such as Christmas and Easter to make your hire arrangements prior to departure through your travel agent. In order to drive in Barbados, you must obtain a local driving licence which costs Bds $10. Take your own driving licence. Several hire operators are authorized to issue these permits. Cars and mini-mokes (small, soft-topped runabouts) are available from a large number of operators and your tour representative or hotel receptionist can assist with information. Not all hire firms take credit cards so check beforehand for acceptability. Normally your car will be delivered to your hotel. Hire cost for a mini-moke is around Bds $90 per day, or Bds $410 per week, and for a small automatic car around Bds $100 per day, or Bds $450 per week. Larger air-conditioned cars cost around Bds $500-600 per week. Prices are inclusive of necessary insurance cover, although you can pay extra to take out collision-damage waiver insurance. Rental firms include Barbados Rent-A-Car, Tudor Bridge, St. Michael, tel: 425-1388, and also at airport, tel: 428-0960; Dears Garage, Bideford House, Browne's Gap, Hastings, Christ Church, tel: 427-7853; Jones Garage Ltd, Passage Rd, St. Michael, tel: 426-4586; Sunset Crest Rent-A-Car, Sunset Crest, St. James, tel: 432-1482; Sunny Isle Motors, 'Dayton', Worthing, Christ Church, tel: 435-7979. Many more are listed in the yellow-pages section of the local telephone directory. See **Accidents & Breakdowns, Driving**.

Chase Vaults: Mystery still surrounds the strange happenings inside the Chase Vaults which are situated in the grounds of the parish church of Christ Church. Lead coffins placed inside the vaults early in the last century were found several times to have moved from their original positions and, despite their tremendous weight, they lay untidily scattered about, one upside down. The door was sealed, and traps laid to catch intruders, but when the vaults were reopened some time later for a further burial the coffins had again been disturbed in a similar way, yet no evidence was found of unauthorized entry. The coffins were removed, and the vault has lain empty since 1820. See **EXCURSION 2**.

Chattel Houses: These small, neat, timber houses, usually set on foundations of loose stones or bricks and often with a veranda to the front, can be seen all over the island. They have been a feature of Barbados since the mid 1800s. After slave emancipation, newly freed people were allowed to build their own houses on land rented from the planters, but as tenants were subject to possible eviction with very little notice it was necessary to design these constructions with mobility in mind. Thus the properties were 'chattel' and could be dismantled, transported and reassembled on a new site very rapidly. Recent legislation making it easier for tenants to buy their properties means that the spectacle of these houses on the move is now rare.

Chemists: See **Pharmacies**.

Cherry Tree Hill: See **St. Nicholas Abbey**.

Children: Barbadians love children and they are assured of much attention wherever they go. Play facilities are, however, very scarce though there is a children's park at Holetown, near Sunset Crest (see **SHOPPING 2**). Some larger hotels offer daily children's programmes but these are reserved for their residents only. Many hotel pools are unsupervised and children are not allowed to use them unless accompanied by parents or guardians. Younger children in particular need as much protection as possible from the fierce rays of the sun, and it is recommended that they should wear a hat during the day (see **Sunbathing**). See **Baby-Sitters**.

Churches: Churches have been present in Barbados since the early 1600s, though most of those which can be seen today were built following the devastating hurricane of 1831 which destroyed many earlier church buildings. There are 11 parish churches, including St. Michael's Cathedral (see **A-Z**) in Bridgetown and this, together with St. George's (see **A-Z**) and St. James (see **A-Z**) parish churches, are the oldest surviv-

St. James Church

ing on the island, all three dating from the late 1700s. Architectural styles vary depending on when built, but Gothic and Georgian influences are evident. A book entitled *Historic Churches of Barbados*, by Barbara Hill and published in Barbados, is an excellent reference work if you are interested.

See **EXCURSIONS**, **WHAT TO SEE**, **Religious Services**.

Climate: Barbados enjoys one of the best and most stable climates in the world with an average of eight or nine hours of sunshine daily. There is little variation in the temperature, which rarely falls below 23°C or rises above 30°C. Sea breezes cool the air. The wettest months are from July to November, the driest February to March. Average relative humidity is around 60-75%. See **Hurricanes**.

Codrington College: This impressive building in the parish of St. John houses an Anglican theology college. Originally the site of a plantation owned by Christopher Codrington, the house and grounds were bequeathed upon his death in 1710 to the Society for the Propagation of the Gospel and for a time between 1875 and 1955 it had close links with the University of Durham. The building, which contains traces of Jacobean architecture, is set in peaceful surroundings and is approached down a long, straight, palm-lined drive. See **EXCURSION 2, WHAT TO SEE 3**.

Complaints: Barbadians are naturally hospitable and keen to make your holiday enjoyable but in the event that you think you have been overcharged, or find that prices do not correspond to those displayed, ask to see the owner or manager of the premises. If you are still not satisfied, then you can report the establishment to the Barbados Tourist Board, tel: 427-2623. Just threatening this course of action should remedy the situation. See **Tourist Information**.

Consulates:
UK – British High Commission: Lower Collymore Rock, St. Michael, tel: 436-6694
Canada – Canadian High Commission: Bishops Court Hill, Pine Rd, St. Michael, tel: 429-3550
US – Embassy: Canadian Imperial Bank Building, Broad St, Bridgetown, tel: 436-4950

Conversion Chart:

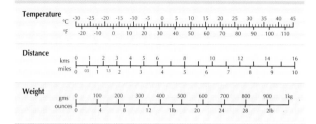

Temperature																
°C	-30	-25	-20	-15	-10	-5	0	5	10	15	20	25	30	35	40	45
°F	-20	-10	0	10	20	30	40	50	60	70	80	90	100	110		

Distance										
kms	0	1	2	3	4	5	6	8	10	12	14	16
miles	0	0.5	1	1.5	2	3	4	5	6	7	8	9	10

Weight										
gms	0	100	200	300	400	500	600	700	800	900	1kg
ounces	0	4	8	12	1lb	20	24	28	2lb	

Credit Cards: See Money.

Crime & Theft: Crime is not a serious problem in Barbados but nevertheless, sensible precautions should be taken. Leave money and valuables in your hotel safe, and take care on the beach to keep everything in sight. In the event of theft contact the police, and ask for a written report for insurance purposes. See **Consulates**, **Emergency Numbers**, **Insurance**, **Police**.

Cruise Passengers: See **Port**.

Currency: The monetary unit is the Barbados Dollar ($) which is linked to the US Dollar at a rate of Bds $1.99 = US $1, though a small commission is usually charged for exchanging currency or traveller's cheques. Paper notes come in the following denominations: $2 (blue); $5 (green); $10 (brown); $20 (mauve); $50 (orange); and $100 (grey). Coin denominations are as follows: $1; 25c; 10c; 5c; 1c. See local newspapers (see **A-Z**) for up-to-date exchange rates. US-dollar notes are accepted in most establishments at a rate of around Bds $1.95 to US $1. See **Money**.

Customs Allowances:

Duty Free Into:	Cigarettes	or Cigars	or Tobacco	Spirits	or Wine
BARBADOS	200	50	230 g	1 *l*	1 *l*
UK	200	50	250 g	1 *l*	2 *l*

Dentists: See **Health**.

Disabled People: Facilities for the disabled are limited and it may be some time before a more satisfactory standard is achieved. In the towns manoeuvrability is difficult owing to narrow pavements, deep drainage gullies and high kerbs. Some parts of the island are hilly and while a few hotels provide ramps many have stairs only, with no lifts. See **Health**, **Insurance**.

Dress Code: Although a relaxed attitude to dress is acceptable from visitors, certain standards are still expected. No nudity or topless bathing is permitted on beaches and when in the city or towns you should not wear bathing costumes. Evening wear requirements for dining out or when visiting nightclubs are generally slightly more formal – the phrase often used is 'elegantly casual', meaning no T-shirts or shorts. Very expensive restaurants and one or two top hotels may expect customers and guests to wear more formal dress, such as a jacket and tie for men and a dress for women, so it is advisable to check on this before arriving.

Drinks: The national drink is rum, which has been distilled in Barbados for hundreds of years to world acclaim. Two of the best

known are Mount Gay and Cockspur. Try a rum punch, or join a Rum Tour (see **Tours**) and become an expert! Other local drinks include fruit punch, fresh coconut water straight from a coconut sliced open for you by a stall-vendor, lime juice, mauby (a bittersweet drink made from boiling pieces of tree bark), and falernum, a liqueur made from almond-flavoured rum and sugar. Banks is the local beer (see **Tours**), and Carlsberg lager is brewed locally. Imported beers from other Caribbean islands are available at reasonable prices but wines and spirits from abroad are expensive.

Drip Stones: Before the days of piped water, drip stones were used to filter supplies taken from springs or wells. At the top of the structure water would be fed into a coral bowl, from where it then filtered through to another hollowed-out coral block beneath and the increasingly cooler water then dripped through that to a vessel at the bottom. Very few examples of complete sets remain in their original locations, though there is one which can be seen at Francia Plantation House (see **EXCURSION 2**, **WHAT TO SEE 4**).

Driving: Barbados is well served with a profusion of some 850 miles
of tarmac roads crisscrossing the island. To drive a car you must be in
possession of a local driving licence (cost $10 Bds) obtainable from the
police on arrival at the airport, from Central Police Station, Bridgetown,
or from selected police stations in the parishes. Some car-hire firms also
are authorized to issue driving licences. You drive on the left-hand side
of the road, but the use of seat belts is not compulsory. Road signs,
which are intermittent on country routes and frequently obscured by
undergrowth, can be confusing for visitors as destinations shown may
point only towards tiny villages. You are therefore recommended to
buy a good map, such as the Ordnance Survey map of Barbados,
which is excellent and is available locally. Free holiday maps are widely distributed, but they contain insufficient detail for more ambitious
exploring. Generally, driving standards are fairly high and courtesy is
extended to visitors in hired cars (identified by the letter 'H' on licence
plates) but other than the new highways, roads are narrow and twisting,
and slow-moving traffic like lorries and donkey carts can be difficult to
overtake. Care and patience are required at all times. Road junctions
can be indistinctly marked and priority at crossroads is not always clear.
Although speed limits nowadays are in kilometres, the vast majority of
people, including children, describe distances in miles! There are four
speed limits: 80 kph on Spring Garden Highway; 60 kph on Adams,
Barrow and Cummings Highways (known as the ABC highways); 50
kph on all other rural roads; and 32 kph in towns and city. Heavy fines
are imposed for breaking speed limits. See **Accidents & Breakdowns,
Bicycle & Motorcycle Hire, Car Hire, Parking, Petrol, Transport.**

Drugs: All drugs are illegal and there are severe penalties for offend-
ers. Contact your embassy or consulate (see **A-Z**) if you are arrested for
a drugs-related offence. A drug-free hot-line operates on 436-5165.

Drug Stores: See **Pharmacies**.

Eating Out: There are dozens of restaurants in Barbados offering a
huge variety of style, service and cuisine. You will find a wide selection
of dishes in Italian, French, Chinese and Indian restaurants in addition

to steak houses, pizza houses, fast-food establishments and snack bars selling local foods and drinks in a variety of backgrounds, ranging from an intimate, romantic setting dining under the stars, to the more boisterous atmosphere of a traditional English pub. It is advisable to make an advance reservation at most restaurants and if you intend paying by credit card check beforehand for acceptability and ask if they have any particular dress requirements. In all cases a 5% Government Tax will be added to your bill, and some restaurants leave tipping to customers' discretion in which case 10-15% should be added, depending on how satisfied you have been with the meal and service. Musical entertainment, from steel bands and folk music to calypso performers and jazz evenings is provided at many restaurants. Prices depend on the standard of food and service in the establishment, but the following price ranges, used in the RESTAURANT pages, are an approximate guide to what you can expect to pay, per person, for dinner excluding wine, tax and tips: Inexpensive – Bds $20-50; Moderate – Bds $50-80; Expensive – Bds $80-120.

See **RESTAURANTS**, **Dress Code**, **Food**, **Tipping**.

Electricity: 110 volts 50 cycle. Small, two-flat-pin plugs are used. If you are coming from the UK your electrical goods will need an adaptor, which can be bought from shops at home or in the airport. Appliances may also need a voltage transformer. American and Canadian appliances can be used without an adaptor.

Emergency Numbers:

Police	tel: 112
Fire	tel: 113
Ambulance	tel: 426-1113
Queen Elizabeth Hospital	tel: 436-6450
Coast Guard	tel: 427-8819
Drug-free hot line	tel: 436-5165

Events: In a part of the world renowned for carnivals Barbados has a good share of colourful festivals which can be celebrated by locals and tourists alike. See local press for details (see **Newspapers**, **What's On**).

February: Holetown Festival, Holetown, St. James, commemorates the anniversary of the first settlement in Barbados in 1627. There is music with colourful parades and dancing. See **Holetown**.

March: Annual Flower Show, Balls Plantation, Christ Church.

Easter: Oistins Fish Festival, Oistins, Christ Church, celebrates the importance of the fishing industry in this part of the island. Events include fishing-boat races, net casting, fish boning and crab racing.

July-August: Crop Over, the biggest festival of the year on Barbados. It celebrates the end of the sugar-cane-cutting season and events take place all over the island, including calypso competitions, street fairs, drama and dance. The final day, known as 'Kadooment', brings everything to a resounding climax with parades, steel bands, calypso and a firework display.

Farley Hill: Now a ruin, this former Great House, which dates from 1818, enjoyed its heyday during the latter half of the 19thC when it was owned by Sir Graham Briggs, a wealthy sugar planter. He extended the property and introduced many new trees and plants to the grounds. Visitors to the house included Queen Victoria's son Prince Alfred, and 18 years later his nephew Prince George (later King George V) spent time there. By 1940, following various changes in ownership, the building had fallen into disrepair, but it was temporarily restored in 1956 as a set for the film *Island in the Sun*, only to be devastated by fire shortly afterwards. Its grounds are now a National Park and open to the public daily (see **PARKS & GARDENS**).

Flower Forest: Opened in 1983, this beautiful 50-acre tropical garden is located in a particularly scenic part of the island. Divided into sections which are linked by pathways, the gardens contain a vast range of flowers, plants and shrubs. A peaceful and tranquil spot, there are ideal photo opportunities not just of the flowers, but of the scenery beyond. The

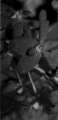

administration building contains a shop and snack bar, and the Forest is open daily. See **EXCURSION 1, MUSTS**.

Food: While you can enjoy international cuisine in many of the island's restaurants, you should try Bajan cookery, which is well worth sampling. Favourite seafood dishes include flying fish, sea egg, crab, shrimp, lobster, red snapper, kingfish, dorado (known locally as dolphin, although it is a fish and not the mammal) and swordfish. Chicken and pork are the

main ingredients in meat dishes, with pepperpot and 'pudding-and-souse' as two popular examples, but bear in mind that servings can contain 'hot' sauces with peppers, spices and seasoning. Cou-cou is a tasty dish made from cornmeal and okra, and other interesting vegetables used in Bajan cooking include plantain, breadfruit, yams, sweet potatoes, cassava, eddoes and christophene. Fruits most commonly found are paw-paw, passion fruit, bananas, mangoes, guavas and, of course, coconut. Good places to find local delicacies are Baxter's Road in Bridgetown (see **NIGHTLIFE, A-Z**) and Atlantis Hotel at Bathsheba (see **MUSTS**). See **RESTAURANTS, Eating Out, Nightlife**.

Garrison Savannah: Around this area are some buildings and arte-facts reflecting the island's military history prior to the withdrawal of British troops in 1905. In front of the Savannah Club, originally the Guard House, is an impressive collection of cannons dating from 1650. The Savannah, now a racecourse, was a parade ground and soldiers were billeted in many of the buildings surrounding it. The present site of the Barbados Defence Force Headquarters accommodated the Drill Hall and behind it was St. Ann's Fort. See **EXCURSION 2, WHAT TO SEE 1**.

Guides: See **Tours, Walks**.

Harrison's Cave: This natural phenomenon of underground cav-erns, streams, waterfalls and pools, discovered nearly 200 years ago,

has only recently been opened to the public. Daily guided tours in open vehicles take visitors on a spectacular one-mile ride through the beautifully illuminated cave system. See **EXCURSION 1, MUSTS**.

Health: Barbados possesses excellent medical facilities and most hotels have a doctor on call. A visiting fee will be payable as well as the cost of any treatment. In an emergency, tel: 426-1113 and ask for an ambulance. The Queen Elizabeth Hospital, tel: 436-6450, has a 24-hr casualty department, and treatment in the public wards is free. Private treatment is also available in private wards but as you will have to pay for this make sure you arrange adequate medical insurance before your trip. If you require dental treatment your hotel or tour representative should be able to recommend a good dentist. You will find a long list of doctors and dentists in the yellow-pages section of the local telephone directory. Although Barbados is free of malaria and other tropical diseases and has a pure water supply, you should ask your travel agent for any up-to-date immunization requirements before you leave. It is advisable to take precautions against the fierce sun by purchasing a suitable blocking lotion (see **Sunbathing**) and as mosquitoes are sometimes present, insect repellent is also useful. See **Disabled People**, **Emergency Numbers**, **Insurance**, **Manchineel Tree**, **Pharmacies**, **Sea Urchins**.

Helicopter Trips: See **Tours**.

Holetown: Situated about halfway up the west coast, Holetown was where the first settlers landed in 1627 following an earlier British expedition in 1625. Barbados remained a British colony for an uninterrupted period right up to independence in 1966. Called Jamestown for a time, it took its current name from the word 'hole', meaning 'a small anchorage'. A memorial erected in 1905 to celebrate the tercentenary of the first landing, mistakenly listed as being 'in 1605' will be found near the police station. St. James Church (see **WHAT TO SEE 2**, **A-Z**) and Folkestone Marine Museum (see **WHAT TO SEE 2**) are in the vicinity. Holetown, now a centre for tourism, contains two shopping malls, restaurants, banks and a supermarket, while the adjoining beach is ideal for snorkelling. See **EXCURSION 1**, **Events**.

Hurricanes: Although Barbados is located in the hurricane zone (the season lasts from June to November), the most violent have passed by the island in recent years and the last direct hit was Hurricane Janet in 1955. A hurricane is defined as occurring when winds of 75 mph are recorded. Thanks to sophisticated modern meteorology, plenty of advance warning is given and regular broadcasts on radio and TV give necessary information and emergency measures. Instructions on what to do in the event of a hurricane warning are normally displayed in hotels, and hurricane shelters are located all over the island.
The local telephone directory contains useful hurricane hints. See **Climate**.

Insurance: Before leaving you are strongly recommended to take out adequate insurance cover against theft and loss of property and money, as well as medical expenses for the duration of your stay. Note that you will probably require extra cover if you intend diving. Your travel agent should be able to assist you to find a suitable policy. See **Crime & Theft**, **Disabled People**, **Driving**, **Health**.

Island Hopping: See **Tours**.

Jolly Roger: This fun-packed excursion on a pirate ship under sail will be enjoyed by all the family, and the party atmosphere is continuous! Daily, four-hour, lunch-time cruises leave from the shallow dock at the harbour at 1000, and you sail up the west coast to a sheltered bay for a full buffet lunch on board. Apart from music for dancing the action includes rope swinging, walking the plank and snorkelling over a wreck. There are also two romantic evening cruises a week, departing at 1800 on Thursday and Saturday and instead of water sports, a leading local band provides live entertainment. A full buffet is served. The cost, at around Bds $85 per person, includes transportation to and from your hotel and all food and drink (except wine and champagne). Children 4-12 years Bds $45, under 4s free. See MUSTS, **Tours**.

Laundries: All the main hotels and apartments have laundries, sometimes with same-day service. Launderettes (known locally as 'laundermats') are coin operated but most will also do service washes for you. They include the following:

Blue Dolphin Laundermat, Free Hill, Black Rock, St. Michael, tel: 424-7590; 0730-1930 Mon.-Sat., 0830-1400 Sun. and bank hol.;

Carlton Laundermat, Carlton Shopping Plaza, Black Rock, St. Michael, tel: 424-1927, 0800-2100 Mon.-Sat., 0800-1500 Sun. and bank hol.;

Hastings Village Laundermat, Balmoral Gap, Hastings, Christ Church, tel: 429-7079; 0800-2100 Mon.-Sat., 0800-1500 Sun.

Many more will be found in the yellow-pages section of the local telephone directory.

Lifeguards: Barbados boasts the oldest life guard service in the Caribbean and there are some 15 stations around the island. Look out for flags coloured red, orange and green which signify safety levels for swimmers. Red means keep out of the water, orange means caution is needed owing to strong currents or tides, and green that it's safe to swim. See BEACHES, **Beaches**.

Local Taxes: Government service tax of 5% is added to bills, and on leaving Barabdos you will have to pay a departure tax of Bds $25.

Lost Property: Report any lost property to your hotel and the local police station. Check lost-and-found columns in the daily newspapers (see **A-Z**).

Manchineel Tree: This tree is found mostly along the beaches of the west coast, and it bears a green fruit resembling a small apple. Under no circumstances should you touch this fruit as not only is it very poisonous if eaten, but it causes blisters when it comes in contact with the skin. Even seeking shelter from rain under the tree is dangerous. Warning notices usually indicate the whereabouts of manchineel trees but if you are in doubt, ask a local inhabitant. If you do come into contact with this tree seek medical advice. See **Health**.

Markets: Market stalls will be found all over the island, with vendors selling anything from fruit and drinks to sweets and shoes. The main markets in Bridgetown are at Fairchild St and Cheapside, and the numerous stalls with their colourful umbrellas in Swan St are worth visiting.

Money: As Barbados dollars are difficult to obtain from British banks, it is advisable to purchase US-dollar traveller's cheques before departure. The Barbados dollar is linked to the US dollar at Bds $1.99 to US $1 though a small commission will probably be charged when converting currency. Many retailers will accept US-dollar traveller's cheques and notes but it is better to pay in local currency, especially when it is possible to bargain for goods. Many hotels will exchange your currency and there is usually only a marginal difference between the rates charged in hotels, shops and banks. Major international credit cards are becoming more widely accepted in many larger stores, some restaurants and several hotels. Some car-hire firms also take credit cards but if you intend paying this way, check with them first for acceptability. Commercial banks in Barbados include: the Bank of Credit and Commerce; Barclays Bank; the Bank of Nova Scotia; the Canadian Imperial Bank of Commerce; the Royal Bank of Canada; and the Barbados National Bank. Most of these have branches throughout the island. Opening times are: 0800-1500 Mon.-Thu.; 0800-1700 Fri. Bank of Nova Scotia and Royal Bank of Canada, all others 0900-1300, 1500-1700; 0900-1300 Sat. Bank of Credit and Commerce. If you should lose credit cards or traveller's cheques, remember to contact the issuing authorities, as well as the police. See **Crime & Theft**, **Currency**.

Mongoose: You are very likely to see these small, furry, long-tailed animals darting across the road as you travel through country roads. They were introduced to Barbados about 100 years ago to control the snake and rat population.

Monkeys: As there are reckoned to be up to 8000 monkeys in Barbados there is a good chance you will see some on your travels around the island. Viewing monkeys at close hand is possible at Barbados Wildlife Reserve (see MUSTS) though no attempt should be made to touch them as they can give a nasty bite.

Music: The importance of music as an ingredient in local culture is best encapsulated in the calypso which has its roots in songs brought centuries ago from Africa by slaves. Nowadays calypsonians use their medium as a vehicle for entertainment, political comment or protest, and the latest songs will be heard blaring from radios or during festivals such as Crop Over (see **Events**). Another local phenomenon is *tuk* bands, which feature instruments such as a tin whistle and two drums, and have origins in both British and African music. Dancers in colourful costumes and a 'tiltman' on stilts often accompany these bands. Steel bands are also popular, their pans being shaped from oildrums, and they play a wide variety of music from classical to popular. The Waterfront Café (see **RESTAURANTS 2**) and After Dark (see **NIGHTLIFE**) have regular evenings of jazz which has a long tradition in Barbados. The Royal Barbados Police Band performs varied programmes at locations all over the island; see newspapers (see **A-Z**) for details of venues. See **NIGHTLIFE**, **Nightlife**.

Nelson, Horatio (1758-1805): Despite Admiral Nelson's established connections with other islands in the Caribbean, he paid few visits to Barbados. His last was in 1805, four months before he was killed in victory at the Battle of Trafalgar. In recognition of his contribution to the defence of the West Indies, a statue was erected in Bridgetown in 1813 to his memory and the surrounding area was named Trafalgar Square. Both remain to this day, predating their London counterparts by some 30 years. See **WHAT TO SEE 1**.

Newspapers: Barbados's daily newspapers, *The Barbados Advocate* and *The Nation*, give good coverage of local and world news. Also published are *The Sunday Sun* and *The Sunday Advocate*. Monthly magazines include *The New Bajan* which carries a supplement, 'What's on in Barbados'. Free papers available in hotels and shops include

The Visitor and *Sun Seeker*, and these give useful tourist information. Most major British and north American newspapers are also available.

Nightlife: Several restaurants, pubs and hotels offer evening entertainment with dancing to local bands. Spectacular shows highlighting cultural heritage in music and dance are held regularly at Plantation Restaurant and at the Barbados Museum. Numerous nightclubs are located in the west and south coastal areas and Bridgetown is a centre for discos, many featuring live bands. Baxter's Road (see **A-Z**) is a popular spot after midnight. See **NIGHTLIFE**, **RESTAURANTS**, **Music**.

Oistins: Situated about five miles east of Bridgetown on the south coast, Oistins (originally called Austin's) is a busy fishing port. The Oistins Fish Festival is held each Easter (see **Events**) and the programme includes fishing boat races, a fish boning competition and exhibitions. See **EXCURSION 2**.

Open House Programme: Organised by the Barbados National Trust (see **A-Z**), this scheme allows access to some of the island's loveliest homes not normally open to the public. The houses are chosen for their architectural interest or decor, and many have impressive grounds and gardens. A perennial favourite is Heron Bay, the home of the late Ronald Tree, which is designed in the style of a classical Italian villa.

The houses are normally open on Wednesdays between mid January and early April by courtesy of the owners. Guided tours and transportation are both available, and information is published in the local press (see **Newspapers**) or you can contact the Barbados National Trust, tel: 426-2421 or 426-9033.

Opening Times: The following are general opening times only which can be subject to variation.
Banks – 0800-1500 Mon.-Thu; 0800-1300, 1500-1700 Fri., except Bank of Nova Scotia and Royal Bank of Canada, 0800-1700 Fri.
Barbados Museum – 0900-1800 Mon.-Sat.
Post Offices – General Post Office, Bridgetown, 0730-1700 Mon.-Fri. Rural branches 0730-1200, 1300-1500 Mon., 0800-1200, 1300-1515 Tue.-Fri.
Stores & boutiques: 0800-1600 Mon.-Fri., 0800-1300 Sat.
Supermarkets: 0800-1800 Mon.-Wed., 0800-1900 Thu. & Fri., 0800-1300 Sat.
Some supermarkets have longer weekend opening hours.

Orientation: Barbados has an area of only 166 square miles so you are never very far from the sea, yet because of the undulating country-side with its deep gullies, rolling hills and network of narrow, twisting roads often bordered by tall sugar-cane fields, it is surprisingly easy to

get lost. A good map is essential and the Ordnance Survey map of Barbados, which includes a street plan of Bridgetown, is available in many local shops and is highly recommended. Free 'holiday maps' are widely distributed in hotels and shops but the keen explorer will require greater detail than is shown in these. In towns, street signs are sometimes indistinct and road direction signs in the country can be confusing, but locals are pleased to assist when necessary.

Parishes: The island is divided into 11 parishes and the boundaries originally laid down in 1645 have barely changed to the present day. Locations and people are always described as being in or from a particular parish, and licence plates on cars indicate in which parish the vehicle is registered.

Parking: Restricted on-street parking in Bridgetown is free but spaces are taken up early in the morning by commuters. There is a multi-storey car park in Chapel Street above the City Centre Mall, and parking costs around Bds $1 per hour. Public car parks, costing around Bds 75c per hour, are located at Independence Sq. (beside the inner basin of the Careenage); off Hinks St (at the mouth of the Careenage); between Temple Yard and Cumberland St where they meet Princess Alice Highway; and off Coleridge St and Roebuck St, both at the northern end of the city. Parking is easier in Holetown, Speightstown and the southern areas where shopping malls are prevalent and offer free parking spaces.

Passports & Customs: An immigration card, normally distributed by your carrier, must be completed before arrival and this, together with a current passport and valid return ticket, should be presented to the immigration officer at the airport. If you require an extension to your stay beyond that granted, application should be made to Immigration and Passports Department, The Wharf, Bridgetown, tel: 426-9912. For visits of no longer than three months, visas are not normally required, though they must be obtained prior to arrival by citizens of the USSR, South Africa, India, Pakistan, China, Cuba and some Eastern European countries. There is no limit to the amount of money that visitors can bring into or take out of Barbados, but import allowances on goods apply.

Allowances for returning residents of the United States are more complex than those shown in the **Customs Allowances** chart, but US $400 of goods at retail value may be taken back if your stay has been longer than 48 hours, provided this facility or any part of it has not been used in the previous 30 days. Duty-free liquor is limited to one litre per person, though paying duty beyond this allowance can still show savings over domestic prices.

A booklet entitled *Tips for Travellers* is available from Barbados Tourist Board offices. See **Customs Allowances**, **Tourist Information**.

Petrol: Petrol stations are located prominently all over the island, and as self-service is not the usual custom, attendants are generally on hand to dispense petrol, clean the windscreen, check oil, tyre pressures etc. Four star costs around Bds $1.30 per litre, but unleaded petrol is not available. Most stations are open seven days (0700-2000 or later Mon.-Sat.; 0700-1900 Sun.).

Pharmacies: Over 70 dispensing chemists, or pharmacies, are spread around the island, the majority being in Bridgetown. They are clearly signed (sometimes using the 'Rx' symbol for medicine) and provide prompt dispensing services. There are no 24-hr pharmacies, but some are open on Sundays and late on certain weekdays: Collins Ltd, Broad St, Bridgetown, tel: 426-4246, is open 0800-1630 Mon.-Fri., 0800-1200 Sat., 0800-1200 Sun. and bank holidays; A.D. Jones, 8 High St, Bridgetown, tel: 426-3241, is open until 1800 on Fri. In case of extreme emergency outside these hours it is possible to have urgent prescriptions dispensed and delivered to you by a pharmacist. The doctor dealing with your case will assist with information and telephone numbers. See **Health**.

Police: Members of the Barbados Police Force are friendly, helpful and well used to answering questions from visitors to the island. They wear a uniform of navy blue trousers with a red stripe running down the outside seam, open-necked grey shirts, a leather belt, and a cap

with a red band. The Royal Barbados Police Band regularly performs at various locations, see newspapers (see **A-Z**) for details. See **Accidents & Breakdowns**, **Crime & Theft**, **Emergency Numbers**.

Port: Passengers arriving on cruise ships are cleared of immigration and customs formalities prior to disembarkation. The passenger terminal building houses shops, some with duty-free facilities, a branch of Barclays Bank where you can exchange currency, and an information desk manned by staff from the Barbados Board of Tourism who will answer your queries. Telephones connecting directly to the New York telephone exchange are available, as are credit card and local pay phones (Bds 25c for five min). International calls can be made from the latter on a reverse-charge or collect-call basis only by dialling 0 for the operator. Ramps and toilet facilities for the disabled are present. A bus service operates from outside the passenger terminal into Bridgetown, and sightseeing tour buses and taxis also leave from here.

Post Offices: The General Post Office is in Cheapside, Bridgetown, and is open 0730-1700 Mon.-Fri. Branches are located in each parish and their hours of opening are 0730-1200, 1300-1500 Mon.; 0800-1200, 1300-1515 Tue.-Fri. Post offices are closed on Saturday and Sunday. Hotel reception desks normally sell stamps and will mail your letters and post cards.
Postal rates: to UK – letters Bds 75c, post cards Bds 50c.;
to USA & Canada – letters Bds 65c, post cards Bds 45c.

Public Holidays: 1 Jan. (New Year's Day); 21 Jan. (Errol Barrow

Day); Good Friday; Easter Monday; first Mon. in May (Labour Day); Whit Monday; first Mon. in Aug. (Kadooment); first Mon. in Oct. (United Nations Day); 30 Nov. (Independence Day); 25 Dec. (Christmas Day); 26 Dec. (Boxing Day).

Rabies: Because Barbados is free of rabies, very strict regulations are in force governing the importation of pets. You can get advice or apply for a permit in advance of your visit from the Ministry of Agriculture, Graeme Hall, Christ Church, tel: 428-4060.

Redlegs: Known also as 'poor whites' they are the descendants of convicted prisoners sentenced by British courts to labour in Barbados for their apparently rebellious activities in the Duke of Monmouth's 1685 rebellion. Many captured supporters of Bonnie Prince Charlie's unsuccessful campaign of 1745-46 were to meet the same unfortunate fate over 60 years later. Having served their sentences as indentured servants, they found themselves socially outcast, unable to mix with the local white population, and in the face of few opportunities to make a living, many lived in poverty. Despite considerable emigration and integration over the years, there are still quite large numbers of poor white people in Barbados, living mainly in the eastern parishes of St. Andrew, St. John and St. Joseph.

Religious Services: A large number of churches are represented in Barbados, and you will find up-to-date information on times of services in local newspapers and magazines. The yellow-pages section of the local telephone directory contains a detailed list of churches all over the island, arranged by denomination, and the following gives an indication of where you can worship:
Anglican – St. Michael's Cathedral, Bridgetown, tel: 429-2421.
0630, 0745, 0900, 1100, 1800 Sun.
Catholic – St. Patrick's Cathedral, Bridgetown, tel: 426-2325.
0700, 0830, 1800 Sun.

Jewish – The Synagogue, Rockley New Rd, Christ Church, tel: 426-5792. 1930 Fri.
Methodist – Bay Street Methodist Church, Bridgetown, tel: 426-2223. 0900, 1800 Sun.
Muslim – Juma Mosque, Kensington New Rd, Bridgetown, tel: 436-2764. Five services daily; special service 1230 Fri.

St. George's Church: Rebuilt in 1784 at a cost of £600 following its destruction in the 1780 hurricane, it contains some interesting sculptures, including work by Westmacott, the man responsible for Nelson's (see **A-Z**) statue in Bridgetown. Also of note is a 1776 painting, *The Resurrection*, by Benjamin West, American-born British painter patronized by King George III for 40 years. See **WHAT TO SEE 4**.

St. James Church: This beautifully restored church at Holetown, where the first settlers landed in 1627, stands on the site of several others which all suffered the ravages of hurricanes over the centuries. While there is some uncertainty as to the exact date of the first building, records indicate the existence of a church in 1660, and it is probable that an earlier building was the first church constructed on the island. The inscription on the bell placed in the north porch reads 'God Bless King William 1696' and predates the American Liberty Bell by some 50 years. The original baptismal font is dated 1684, and some of the church silver dates from 1682. Many of the original settlers are buried in the church and churchyard. See **EXCURSION 1**, **WHAT TO SEE 2**, **Churches**.

St. John's Church: There have been several buildings on the site of the present church which dates from 1836. It contains a Westmacott sculpture and a beautifully carved pulpit, while in the churchyard is the grave of Ferdinand Paleologus, descendent of the brother of Constantine, the last Byzantine emperor, killed in Constantinople in 1453. The church is located on high ground, affording excellent views along the east coast. See **EXCURSION 2**, **WHAT TO SEE 3**, **Churches**.

St. Michael's Cathedral: The first church on the present site dates

St. George's Church

St. Michael's Cathedral

from 1665 and from then until its demolition in the hurricane of 1780 there were constant structural problems and seemingly endless difficulties caused by acts of man and God! By 1786 at a cost of £10,000 a new church had been built and even then more problems arose, particularly with the roof, and yet the whole building survived the devastating hurricane of 1831 along with only two others, St. George's and St. James, all remaining in use to the present day. St. Michael's was elevated to cathedral status in 1825. See **WHAT TO SEE 1**, **Churches**.

St. Nicholas Abbey: This is not an abbey, but one of the oldest plantation houses and estates in Barbados. A private dwelling house (though open to the public Mon.-Fri.), St. Nicholas dates from around 1650 and was built in fine Jacobean style, though its design curiously includes chimneys and fireplaces! Much of the roof is original, and the house contains many antiques, including a Sheraton sideboard. A film shot in the '30s and shown twice a day gives a fascinating glimpse of the plantation at work and also includes scenes of the sea voyage from

England. The estate of some 420 acres still produces sugar as it has since 1640, and the lands include Cherry Tree Hill, reached from St. Nicholas by a road lined with ancient mahogany trees. The views from Cherry Tree Hill towards the east coast are magnificent. See **EXCURSION 1, WHAT TO SEE 2**.

Sam Lord's Castle: Although it is now part of a hotel complex, this majestic Regency mansion has been carefully restored and maintained by its present owners. Built by Sam Lord in the early part of the 19thC, the rich abundance of style, design and content contrasts sharply with his reputation as a rascal and malefactor. Popular legend has it that Sam Lord caused many wrecks on nearby Cobblers Reef by hanging out lanterns at night to deceive ships into thinking they had reached Bridgetown, but while evidence does not support this, there is little doubt as to his duplicity in other matters.
See **EXCURSION 2, WHAT TO SEE 4**.

A-Z

Sea Urchins: These brittle creatures, found on beaches or in the sea, are covered in sharp needles which break off when trodden upon and become embedded in the skin. Locals, well used to this minor but painful inconvenience, find relief in the application of hot candle wax to the affected area and they are usually willing to lend assistance if asked politely.

Shopping: The largest congregation of shops, stores and boutiques is in the Broad St area of Bridgetown, and in addition some bigger stores have branches in the many shopping centres throughout the island, and around the west and south coasts in particular. Items for sale include cameras, crystal, watches, jewellery, china, silks, perfumery, tobacco, spirits and British woollen and tweed clothing. Some goods can be purchased duty-free for immediate use. Locally handcrafted products made from coral, wood, leather, straw, shell and clay are found everywhere, but the Pelican Village complex in Bridgetown (see **SHOPPING 1**) particularly is worth a visit. You can bargain for items sold by beach vendors. As a general rule, most shops and stores in Bridgetown are open 0900-1600 Mon.-Fri., 0900-1300 Sat., although some stores have longer trading hours. See **SHOPPING**, **Arts & Crafts**, **Best Buys**, **Markets**, **Opening Times**.

Signal Stations: Of the six constructed between 1818 and 1819 only two survive in any recognisable form: Gun Hill (see **EXCURSION 2, WHAT TO SEE 4**) and Cotton Tower (see **EXCURSION 1, WHAT TO SEE 3**), both being in the care of the Barbados National Trust (see **A-Z**). Originally built for security purposes, they enabled communications to be sent by flag signals or semaphore to all parts of the island instantly, a big improvement on earlier methods of sending notes by messenger on horseback. Later uses included announcing the arrival of shipping, warning of approaching hurricanes, and advising children that it was time to go to school! Below Gun Hill, carved out of solid coral, is a huge lion with its paw resting on a globe symbolizing the world, and the Latin inscription beneath eulogises Britain's imperial domination of the time. It was sculpted by a Captain Wilkinson of the Norfolk Regiment in 1868.

Smoking: Smoking is forbidden on all buses and in some taxis and is generally not allowed in the majority of shops and stores. Locally rolled Havana cigars cost around Bds $25-35 for five.

Speightstown: Situated on the west coast about ten miles north of Bridgetown, Speightstown was at one time known as Little Bristol because of the huge volume of trade it had with the English city. It was founded by William Speight, a member of Barbados's first parliament, in 1639. Despite the town's changing fortunes through the centuries, some of its old three-storey buildings with galleries remain. The town is well served with a large supermarket, department store and a good range of shops. See **EXCURSION 1, SHOPPING 2**.

Sports: The biggest spectator sport is cricket, widely accepted as Barbados's national religion. Played all year round on village greens, beaches and parks, the main test-match season falls between January and April, with games being staged at Kensington Oval in Bridgetown. Details of both local games and test matches are broadcast on television and radio (see **A-Z**), and published in newspapers (see **A-Z**). Also popular is horse racing from the Garrison Savannah (see **A-Z**), and meetings are held every month except May and October. Entry to

Gun Hill

grandstand costs Bds $10 and Bds $5 to field stand. For something different, goat races and even crab races are held occasionally in different parts of the island – see press and radio for details. Participatory sports include all water sports (see **A-Z**), golf, walking (see **Walks**), horse riding, tennis, squash and cycling (see **Bicycle & Motorcycle Hire**). See **SPORTS & ACTIVITIES**.

Sunbathing: While the climate in Barbados is most agreeable, it is always worth bearing in mind that in tropical regions the sun is very fierce, and sensible precautions should be taken to avoid over-exposure. During the first few days limit sunbathing to 15 min per day, and build this up only gradually, avoiding the most intense period between 1100-1500 hours. Buy a suitable sun-blocking cream and re-apply it frequently as you will perspire. It's also a good idea to wear a hat. If you do suffer from sunburn, a pharmacist (see **A-Z**) will recommend a soothing lotion but in severe cases contact a doctor without delay. See **Children**, **Health**.

Sunbury Plantation House: A private dwelling, this 300-year-old plantation house provides a unique insight into its past through a superb display of fine antiques, maps, prints and documents. The collection also includes an interesting range of horse-drawn carriages and other traditional vehicles. The roguish Sam Lord (see **Sam Lord's Castle**) was a regular visitor to Sunbury, and his personal decanter and glasses are on view. See **EXCURSION 2**, **WHAT TO SEE 4**.

Sandy Lane Bay

Taxis: As there are around 1000 taxis on the island, finding one is relatively easy. Ranks are located at many hotels, at the airport, at the harbour and in Bridgetown, particularly around the Careenage area (see **WHAT TO SEE 1**). If you do have difficulty in getting a taxi, your hotel receptionist will telephone for one. Taxis are identified by the letter 'Z' on the licence plate, and a 'Taxi' sign on the roof. Though they are not metered, fixed fares do apply for certain destinations. Displays of fare structures will be found at the airport and some hotels, and they are published in free newspapers such as *The Visitor* (see **Newspapers**). It is very important that you establish the fare with the driver before you commence your journey, and this particularly applies to sightseeing or round-the-island trips. As a maximum of four people can travel together, sharing a taxi will reduce your costs.

Some sample fares are as follows:

from the airport to: Speightstown Bds $42; Holetown Bds $30; Crane Bds $18.

from Bridgetown to: Harrison's Cave Bds $24; Bathsheba Bds $38; airport Bds $26; North Point Bds $35.

Telephones & Telegrams: Local calls from private telephones are free. Public phone booths are positioned all over the island and local calls cost Bds 25c for five minutes. Though you cannot dial overseas numbers directly from these phones, collect calls can be made through the operator (dial 0). You can normally make overseas calls or send telegrams from your hotel by arrangement, but a surcharge is usually levied for this service. Alternatively, overseas calls can be made from the offices of Barbados External Telecommunications Ltd (BET), at Carlisle House, Bridgetown, tel: 426-3178, or at Wildey just outside the city, tel: 427-5200. Faxes and cables can also be sent from these offices. Calls to the UK, USA and Canada cost around Bds $3.30 per minute peak time (Mon.-Sat. 0700-2300) and $2.85 Bds per minute off-peak (Mon.-Sat. 2300-0700 and all day Sun.). Check with the operator for the latest charge rates. To phone the UK direct, dial 011-44 followed by the area code (omitting 0 when it's the first digit) and number. To call the USA and Canada, dial 1 followed by area code and number. Cardphones are located at BET's Bridgetown office, the harbour and the

airport. Phonecards in denominations of Bds $10, $20 and $40 can be purchased at Cardphone sites.

Overseas-rates information	0
Assistance in dialling	0
Directory enquiries	119

Television & Radio: Six radio stations broadcast from three operators; they are as follows: CBC Radio (900kHz AM); Voice of Barbados (790kHz AM); Liberty Radio (98.1 FM); Yess 10/4 (104 FM); Barbados Broadcasting Service (90.7 FM); and Star Radio (Radioffusion). CBC-TV operates the only television station (Channel 9). Their programmes include daily broadcasts from the Cable News Network (CNN). Three subscription television channels provide programmes on education, sports and entertainment.

Time Difference: Barbados time is four hours behind GMT, therefore during British Summer Time it is five hours behind. It is one hour ahead of US Eastern Standard Time.

Tipping: It is customary to leave a 10% tip or even 15% if you are particularly pleased with the standard of service provided, though most restaurants, cafés and hotels will add a service charge to your bill. Porters expect around Bds $1 per bag, and taxi drivers between Bds $2 and Bds $5 depending on the length of journey. For a fortnight's stay a tip of around Bds $20 would be appreciated by your room maid.

Toilets: Public toilets are scarce, even around popular tourist locales such as beaches or in towns. However, hotels, restaurants or department stores are unlikely to be far away and the facilities in such places will normally be available to you. Generally the standard of hygiene is good.

Tourist Information: The Board of Tourism's offices in Bridgetown are located in Harbour Road, tel: 427-2623, and they are open 0815-1630 Mon.-Fri. They can answer your queries and provide maps, brochures and leaflets on the wide choice of attractions available. Information booths are also located at the harbour passenger terminal and at the airport. Free newspapers such as *The Sun Seeker* and *The Visitor* are aimed at the tourist, and provide much useful information. The Barbados Board of Tourism also has offices abroad: in London, at 263 Tottenham Court Rd, W1P 9AA, tel: 071-636 9448; in Toronto, at Suite 1508, 20 Queen St West, M5H 3R3, tel: 416-979 2137; and in New York, at 800 Second Ave, 10017, tel: 212-986 6516, as well as in Montreal, Los Angeles and Frankfurt. See **Accommodation**, **Tours**, **What's On**.

Tours: A variety of organized guided tours to sights around Barbados is operated by several companies, and details can be obtained from the Board of Tourism (see **Tourist Information**), your hotel reception desk or your tour representative. Bus tours, taxi tours, helicopter trips, boat trips, tours to other islands, a rum tour and even a submarine voyage are all available, and the following is only a selection.

Bus tours – there are many to choose from, of varying duration. All-day tour prices are usually inclusive of lunch and entry fees to places of interest and cost from Bds $80 per person. Most buses are comfortable, and a guide, equipped with microphone, provides commentary. Trips around Bridgetown, nature tours and round-the-island tours are available, and operators include: L¸E. Williams Tour Co. Ltd, tel: 427-1043; Paul Foster Travel, tel: 426-5160; Johnson's Stable & Garage Ltd, tel: 426-4205; and Remac Tours, tel: 422-0546.

Taxi tours – can be arranged directly with the driver who will suggest an itinerary but, as taxis are not metered, it is important that you agree the price of your excursion before you set out. Cost will depend on length and duration of the journey, but around Bds $180 for a day is normal. This, of course, can be split between up to four people.

Helicopter island tours – a novel if rather expensive way to see Barbados. A 20-min trip costs around Bds $150 per person, but the views are wonderful. For bookings and enquiries, tel: 431-0069 or 435-8593.

Boat trips – several firms offer skippered charter cruises and your hotel will provide information. For something different, become a pirate and take a cruise on the *Jolly Roger*. Daily lunch-time cruises leave from the shallow dock at the harbour at 1000, returning at 1400. As you cruise up the coast, lunch and drinks (all included in the cost) are served and snorkelling over a wreck, walking the plank, and rope swinging are all part of the action! Evening cruises feature live entertainment and dancing. The all-inclusive price is Bds $85 per person; 4-12 years Bds $45; under 4s free. See MUSTS, **A-Z**.

Island hopping – neighbouring islands such as Dominica, Martinique, Mustique, St. Lucia and Grenada are only a short flight away and one-day trips can easily be arranged. Fly-sail combinations to the Grenadines are also available. Contact Safari Tours Ltd for information and prices, tel: 428-2474.

Rum tours – take place every Wednesday around midday and the price

includes transportation to and from your hotel, a buffet lunch and a guided tour around the West India Rum Refinery, home of Cockspur Rum, with steel-band music and rum tasting. The cost is around Bds $55 per person; for reservations, tel: 435-6900.

Free guided tours are available at the Mount Gay Refinery, St. Lucy, at 1100 and 1400 Mon.-Fri.; closed public holidays. See **EXCURSION 1, Drinks**.

Submarine trip – the submarine *Atlantis II* makes both day and night-time trips to explore coral reefs, sponge gardens and wrecks, and to observe the abundance of marine life to be found in waters up to a depth of 150 ft. Trips last for one hr and large viewports ensure you miss none of the spectacle. The cost is approximately Bds $140 per person. For information and reservations, tel: 436-8929. See **MUSTS**.

Brewery tour – free guided tours around Banks Brewery operate 1000 Tue., 1000 & 1300 Thu. For further information, tel: 429-2113.

Transport: You will have no difficulty in getting around the island as

cars, mini-mokes (small, soft-topped runabouts), bicycles and scooters are all available for hire by the day or week. A good bus service operates, and there are plenty of taxis. See **Airport**, **Bicycle & Motorcycle Hire**, **Buses**, **Car Hire**, **Driving**, **Taxis**, **Tours**.

Traveller's Cheques: See **Money**.

Turner's Hall Woods: Prior to its settlement in 1627, Barbados was covered in thick tropical forest and Turner's Hall is the only area which still has its original vegetation, as it would have been found by the first settlers. It is a difficult place to get to, requiring a lengthy walk, but once there you will find dense foliage and numerous varieties of rare trees, shrubs and plants, some belonging uniquely to these woods. Tree species include macaw palm, cabbage palm, silk-cotton tree, locust tree, and the jack-in-the-box tree. Monkeys inhabit the woods, as do large numbers of birds. See **PARKS & GARDENS**.

Villa Nova: Built in 1834, Villa Nova is one of the finest plantation Great Houses in Barbados, and is today open to the public at set times. It is a private dwelling containing many fine antiques and standing in 12 peaceful acres of woodland and gardens. It was owned between 1965 and 1971 by the late Earl of Avon, Sir Anthony Eden, former British Prime Minister, who used it as his winter residence. See **EXCURSION 2**, **WHAT TO SEE 3**.

Walks: Guided walks sponsored by the Barbados National Trust (see **A-Z**) take place each Sunday at 0600 sharp, and there are also afternoon walks at 1530. They are divided into three categories: fast walks for those primarily wanting exercise, the medium for those who can't keep up with the fast types, and the stop-and-stare category – ideal if you want to enjoy a more leisurely pace with time to learn about the island's history, flora and fauna. Comfortable walking shoes should be worn and loose clothing such as a T-shirt and shorts or slacks is recommended. Take a hat and your camera, too. Starting points vary each week, and details are available from Barbados National Trust, tel: 426-2421. See **SPORTS & ACTIVITIES 3**.

Water Sports: Barbados is famous for its excellent water-sports facilities and there is an abundance of choice, from scuba diving for beginners to parasailing. In general terms the west-coast waters of the Caribbean Sea are calmer than those around the south, and consequently they are ideal for waterskiing, sailing, swimming, snorkelling, diving and parasailing. However, if you are interested in windsurfing, the slightly rougher seas and steady breezes along the south coast provide excellent conditions. The Atlantic rollers and currents along the east coast mean that the seas there are very rough and surfers flock to the Bathsheba area (see **WHAT TO SEE 3**) in particular for their sport. Swimming is possible only at a few sheltered spots. Water-sports centres offering a variety of pursuits are located at many of the large hotels along the west and south coasts.

Cruise operators will be found at the Careenage in Bridgetown, and a five-hour cruise will cost around Bds $100 per person, including food and drinks. Deep-sea fishing charters also operate from the Careenage. Glass-bottom-boat trips are popular, enabling views of marine life, reefs and wrecks at close quarters. Scuba-diving lessons and equipment hire are widely available at water-sports centres, and sailing craft, sailboards, snorkels, masks and fins can also be hired. See **SPORTS & ACTIVITIES 1 & 2**.

What's On: Your hotel should be a good source of advice, and the daily newspapers carry up-to-date information, as do free papers such as *The Visitor*, *Sun Seeker* and the monthly free supplement, 'What's on in Barbados', which comes with *The New Bajan* magazine. The Barbados Tourist Board, Harbour Rd, Bridgetown, tel: 427-2623, with branches at the airport and harbour, will also provide information. Tuning in to local radio stations can also be useful. See **Newspapers**, **Television & Radio**, **Tourist Information**.

Whistling Frogs: First-time visitors to Barbados are often mystified by a chorus of whistling sounds alongside the more familiar hissing of crickets during the hours of darkness, and this curious noise is made by a tiny frog, less than three quarters of an inch in size!